# Data Scientist

## Roadmap

## A Comprehensive Guide

By: Mohammed M.Ahmed

Data Scientist Roadmap

Copyright © 2024 Mohammed M.Ahmed

# DEDICATION

To my parents, who have always been by my side.

To my wife, who helps me during my life journey.

To my kids, who lighten up my life.

# Contents

# Data Scientist Roadmap

# ACKNOWLEDGMENTS

I express my gratitude to my instructors for their unwavering assistance while writing this book.

I am deeply indebted to my family for their tireless support and for enduring the inconveniences while I worked on the Book.

# Chapter 1

# Introduction

Welcome to **"Data Scientist Roadmap: A Comprehensive Guide"** This book is designed to be your gateway into the world of data science, providing a smooth, clear, and accessible path for beginners and students aspiring to become data scientists. Whether you are just starting your journey or looking to solidify your foundational knowledge, this guide offers the easiest and most effective ways to navigate the field.

This book stands out for the way it lays out a roadmap for the reader to follow from the very beginning to the end of data science, what sets this book apart is its focus on making complex concepts understandable through clear explanations and attractive illustrative figures. Each chapter is designed to pave the roadmap for learners, ensuring that even the most intricate topics are presented in an approachable manner. The use of visual aids is a key feature, as these sketches and figures help clarify concepts and make the learning process more engaging and less overwhelming.

This book is structured to serve as your first step towards mastering data science, covering a wide range of essential topics. You'll find chapters on mathematics, statistics and probabilities, machine learning, deep learning, natural language processing (NLP), and programming languages. Each section provides a thorough understanding of the subject, equipping you with the knowledge needed in the field.

In addition to foundational knowledge, the book offers valuable recommendations and instructions to guide your learning process. These insights are intended to help you not only understand the theoretical aspects but also apply them in practical scenarios. This book can be your companion in various data science projects, providing guidance and support as you work through real-world problems.

A multitude of resources have been utilized to create this comprehensive guide, aiming to be a valuable reference for both learners and researchers. By focusing on clarity and understanding, we hope to provide a solid foundation for anyone looking to embark on a data science journey. With fewer words and more insightful illustrations, this book aims to make your learning experience both informative and enjoyable.

## 1.1 Artificial Intelligence vs. Machine Learning vs. Data Science

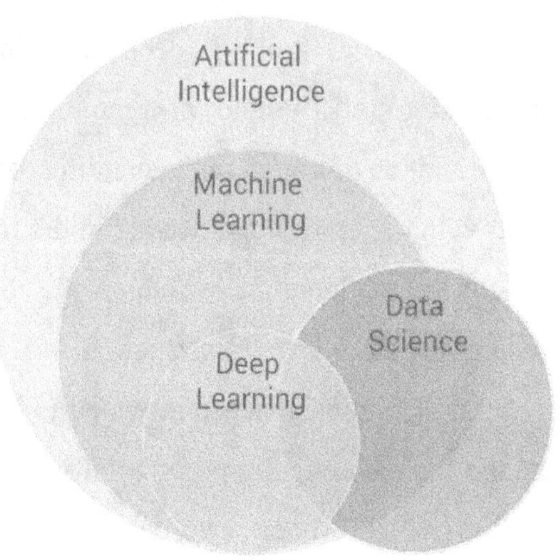


Machine Learning (ML), Data Science (DS), and Artificial Intelligence (AI) are interconnected fields that often overlap, but each has distinct focuses and applications. Here's a concise breakdown to clarify their differences and relationships:

## 1.1.1  Artificial Intelligence (AI)

**Definition:** Artificial Intelligence refers to the broad science of mimicking human abilities. AI systems are designed to perform tasks that typically require human intelligence, such as visual perception, speech recognition, decision-making, and language translation.

**Key Areas**

- **Artificial narrow intelligence (ANI):** Specialized systems that perform specific tasks, such as virtual assistants like Siri or recommendation systems.
- **Artificial general intelligence (AGI):** Hypothetical systems that can perform any intellectual task that a human can. These systems do not yet exist.
- **Artificial superintelligence (ASI):** which is more capable than a human. These systems do not yet exist.

### Techniques

- Rule-Based Systems
- Expert Systems
- Machine Learning

### Applications

- Computer Vision
- Robotics
- Game Playing
- Natural Language Processing (NLP)

## 1.1.2   Machine Learning (ML)

**Definition:** Machine Learning is a subset of AI focused on developing algorithms that allow computers to learn from and make predictions based on data. Instead of being explicitly programmed, ML systems improve their performance through experience.

# Types of ML

- ❑ **Supervised Learning:** Models are trained in labeled data. Common algorithms include linear regression, decision trees, and support vector machines.

- ❑ **Unsupervised Learning:** Models find patterns and relationships in unlabeled data. Techniques include clustering (e.g., K-means) and association analysis.

- ❑ **Reinforcement Learning:** Models learn by interacting with an environment and receiving rewards or penalties. They are used in robotics and game-playing.

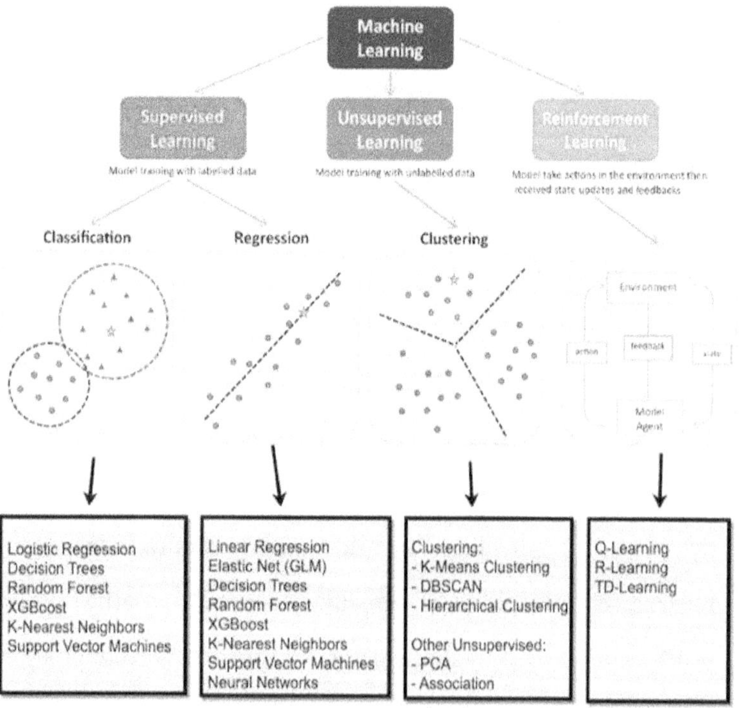

## Key Concepts

- Training and Testing Data
- Overfitting and Underfitting
- Feature Selection and Engineering

## Applications

- Fraud Detection
- Recommendation Systems
- Predictive Maintenance
- Autonomous Vehicles

# 1.1.3  Data Science (DS)

**Definition:** Data Science is an interdisciplinary field that uses scientific methods, processes, algorithms, and systems to extract insights and knowledge from structured and unstructured data. It encompasses a variety of techniques from statistics to computer science, and information theory.

## Components

- **Data Collection and Cleaning:** Gathering and preparing data for analysis.
- **Exploratory Data Analysis (EDA):** Summarizing the main characteristics of data, often using visual methods.
- **Statistical Analysis and Modeling:** Applying statistical methods to identify patterns or relationships.

- **Machine Learning:** Applying ML algorithms to build predictive models.
- **Data Visualization:** Creating visual representations of data to communicate insights effectively.

## Key Tools

- Programming Languages: Python, R
- Data Visualization Tools: Tableau, Matplotlib
- Big Data Technologies: Hadoop, Spark
- Databases: SQL, NoSQL

## Applications

- Business Intelligence
- Healthcare Analytics
- Social Media Analysis
- Market Research

## Interconnections

### AI and ML:

ML is a core subset of AI. While AI encompasses the broader goal of creating systems that can perform tasks that require human intelligence, ML provides the statistical and algorithmic tools to achieve these capabilities.

### ML and DS:

Data Science uses ML algorithms to analyze and predict outcomes from data. ML is a crucial component of the Data

Science toolkit, enabling data scientists to build models that can learn from data and make predictions.

❑ **AI and DS:**

Data Science supports AI development by providing the necessary data and analytical tools to create intelligent systems. Conversely, AI techniques can enhance Data Science by automating data processing and generating deeper insights.

## 1.2 Data Science life cycle

The Data Science Lifecycle outlining the sequential steps involved in a data science project:

- ◉ **Business Understanding:** This initial phase consists of identifying the problem that needs solving. It requires asking relevant questions and defining clear objectives.

- ◉ **Data Mining:** In this phase, data is gathered and extracted from various sources for the project. This step is crucial for obtaining the necessary data to analyze.

- ◉ **Data Cleaning:** This step addresses any inconsistencies or missing values in the data. Clean data is essential for accurate analysis and model building.

- **Data Exploration:** Here, data is visually analyzed to form hypotheses and understand patterns, trends, and relationships within the data. This exploration guides further analysis.

- **Feature Engineering:** Important features are selected, and new ones are created from the raw data. This step helps to make the data more meaningful for the model.

- **Predictive Modeling:** Machine learning models are trained using cleaned and engineered data. These models are then evaluated for their performance and used to make predictions.

- **Data Visualization:** Finally, the findings are communicated to stakeholders using plots and interactive visualizations, making the insights clear and actionable.

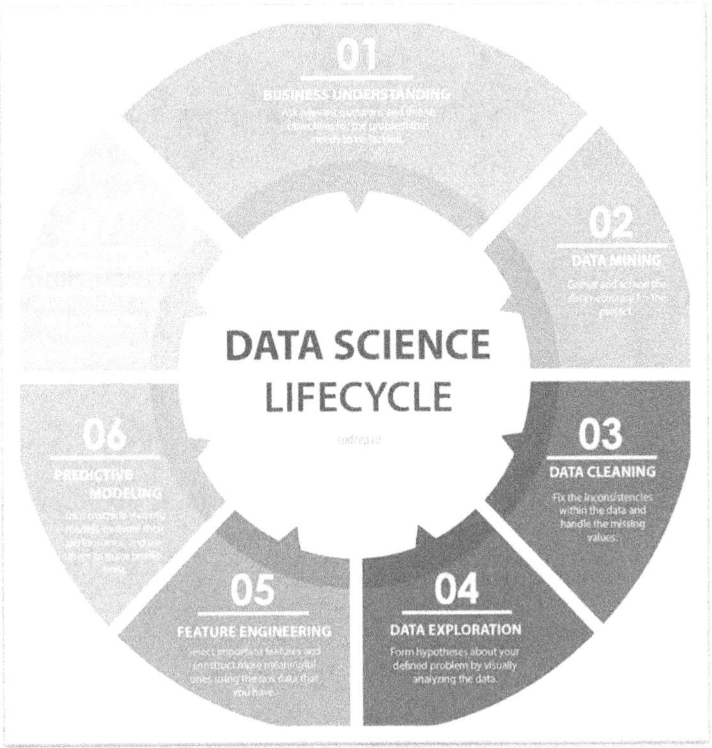


## 1.3 Data Science RoadMap

A roadmap to becoming a data science expert, emphasizing the key areas of learning and development:

- ⊙ **Start with Fundamentals:** The journey begins with mastering the basics, including mathematics, Python programming, data structures, and SQL. These foundational skills are essential for understanding more complex concepts.
- ⊙ **Specialize in Core Areas**

- **Data Engineering:** Focus on hypothesis testing, data processing, and storage. This area is crucial for handling large volumes of data efficiently.

- **Data Analytics:** Engage in exploratory data analysis (EDA) and data visualization. This step helps to derive meaningful insights and understand data trends.

- **Machine Learning:** Develop expertise in machine learning algorithms, neural networks, and deep learning. These are critical for building predictive models and solving complex data problems.

- **Deployment:** Learn to deploy models and solutions in real-world environments using tools like Docker and Kubernetes, along with web development skills. This step ensures that models can be effectively integrated into practical applications.

- **Achieve Data Science Expertise:** By mastering these areas and working on real-world projects, one can become a data science expert, capable of tackling advanced data challenges and creating impactful solutions.

This roadmap provides a structured path, guiding learners from basic skills to advanced data science expertise.

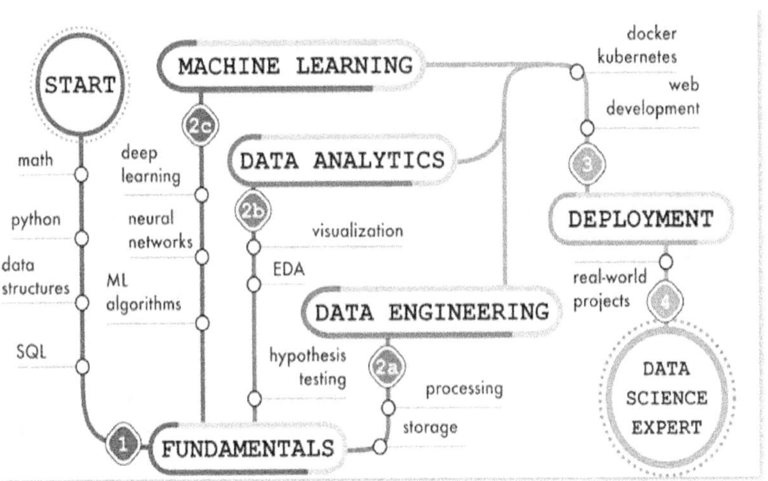


Data scientists can better understand the key concepts by referring to the Figure below, which depict the data science roadmap.

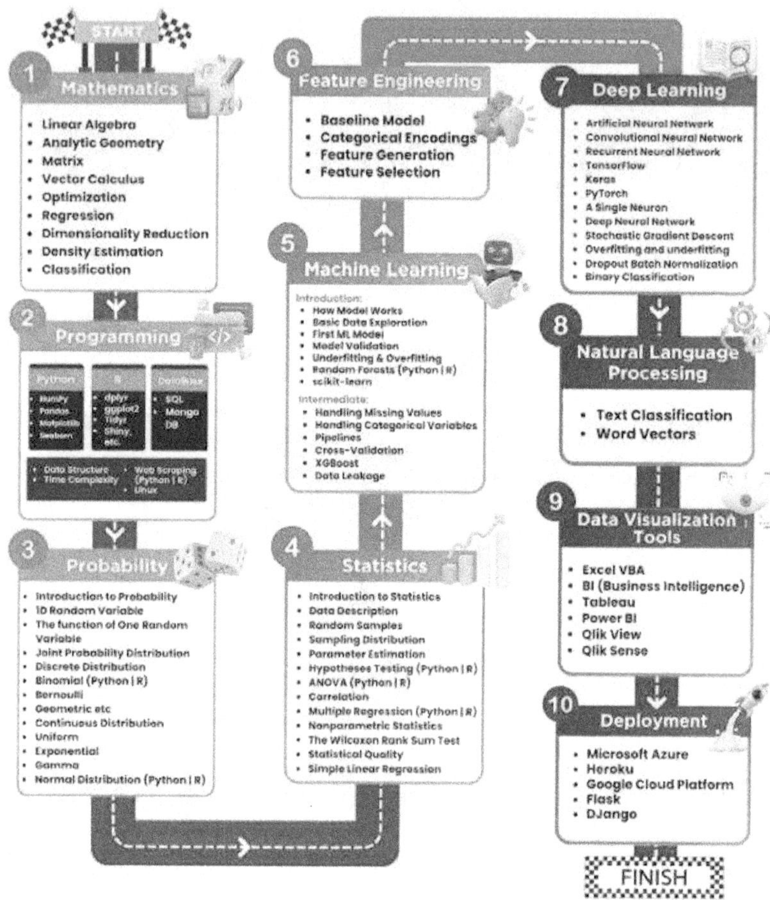


## 1.4 Data Analyst vs. Data Scientist vs. Data Engineer

# Data Analyst

**Role:** Data analysts, rather obviously, analyze data. They do it to identify patterns and come up with actionable insights. These patterns and insights are presented in the reports and dashboards, enabling decision-makers to make informed decisions.

Data analysts are mostly tasked with descriptive (What happened?) and diagnostic (Why did it happen?) data analysis.

**Key Responsibilities**

- ❏ **Data Cleaning:** Preparing data for analysis by standardizing it, changing its format, and dealing with duplicates, missing values, and data inconsistencies.

- ❏ **Data Analysis:** Using statistical methods to understand trends, patterns, and insights in data.

- ❏ **Data Visualization and Reporting**: Communicating data analysis findings through reports, data visualizations, and dashboards.

## Data Scientist

**Role Summary:** Data scientists also analyze data but on a more advanced level. They use statistical models and machine learning algorithms to determine the likelihood of future events. Unlike data analysts, this tells us they are concerned with predictive (What will happen?) and prescriptive (What should be done?) data analysis.

**Key Responsibilities**

- ❏ **Advanced Analytics:** Using advanced statistical techniques to extract insights from data.

- ❏ **Machine Learning:** Implementing machine learning algorithms to learn from the existing data.

- **Predictive Modeling:** Building and deploying models to predict future events on the actual and new data.

These key responsibilities are built on the same work that data analysts do. Data scientists also can't do without **data cleaning** and **data visualization**.

# Data Engineer

Role Summary: Data engineers are responsible for designing, building, and maintaining the systems and architecture that allow data to be collected, stored, and analyzed. They ensure that data is accessible, reliable, and prepared for further analysis by data analysts and data scientists.

**Key Responsibilities**

- **Data Pipeline Development:** Creating and managing data pipelines to extract, transform, and load (ETL) data from various sources into a data warehouse or other storage systems.

- **Data Architecture:** Designing and implementing scalable data architectures that support the organization's data needs, ensuring data is stored efficiently and securely.

- **Data Integration:** Integrating data from diverse sources, including databases, APIs, and third-party platforms, to ensure consistency and usability.

❑ **Data Quality Management:** Monitoring data quality, integrity, and accuracy, and implementing measures to improve data reliability.

❑ **Performance Optimization:** Optimizing the performance of data systems and databases to ensure efficient data retrieval and processing.

❑ **Collaboration:** Working closely with data analysts, data scientists, and other stakeholders to understand their data needs and provide the necessary infrastructure and support.

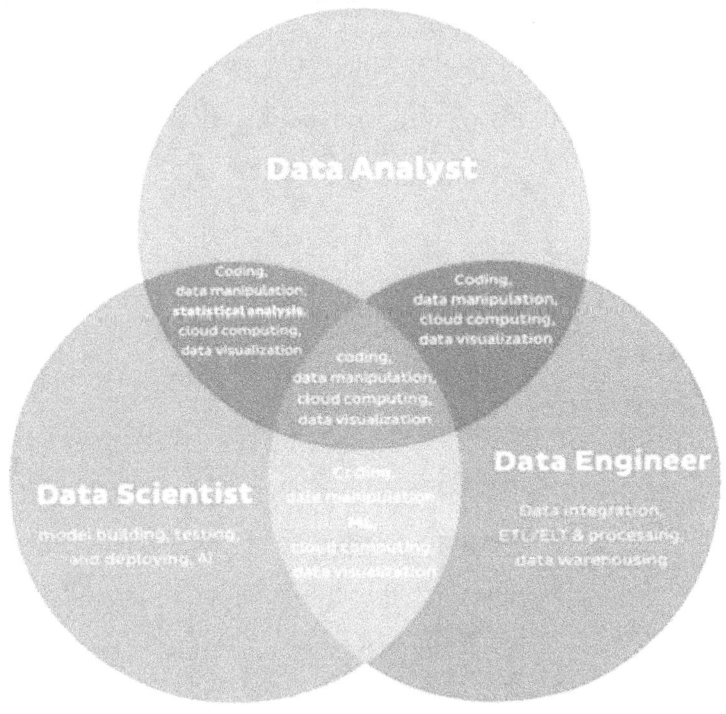

## 1.5  Data Science Roles and How They Interact

The intersection of roles and skills between Data Engineers, Data Scientists, and Business Stakeholders within a data-driven organization:

## Data Engineer

- **Core Skills**: Data ingestion (ETL tools), database systems, Hadoop ecosystem, data APIs, data modeling, and data warehousing.
- **Responsibilities**: They focus on collecting, managing, analyzing, and visualizing data. They also build and deploy data infrastructure and architecture.

## Data Scientist

- **Core Skills**: Proficiency in Python, R, distributed computing, machine and deep learning, feature engineering, predictive modeling, statistics, math, storytelling, and data visualization.
- **Responsibilities**: Data scientists ascribe value to raw data through interpretation and modeling, using sophisticated methods to interrogate the data. They develop hypotheses, test variables, and provide insights that drive decision-making.

## Business Stakeholder

- **Core Skills**: Critical thinking, business intelligence, statistics, math, data stewardship, financial analysis, value chains, ROI, NPV, domain expertise, and communication.

- **Responsibilities**: Stakeholders focus on journey mapping, value streams, services maps, and deployment and integration. They ensure that data efforts align with business goals, focusing on monetization, governance, and hypothesis development.

The overlap in the Venn diagram illustrates shared competencies, such as analysis, programming, big data, and the ability to bridge technical and business domains. This collaboration ensures that data initiatives are technically sound, aligned with business strategy, and ultimately deliver value.

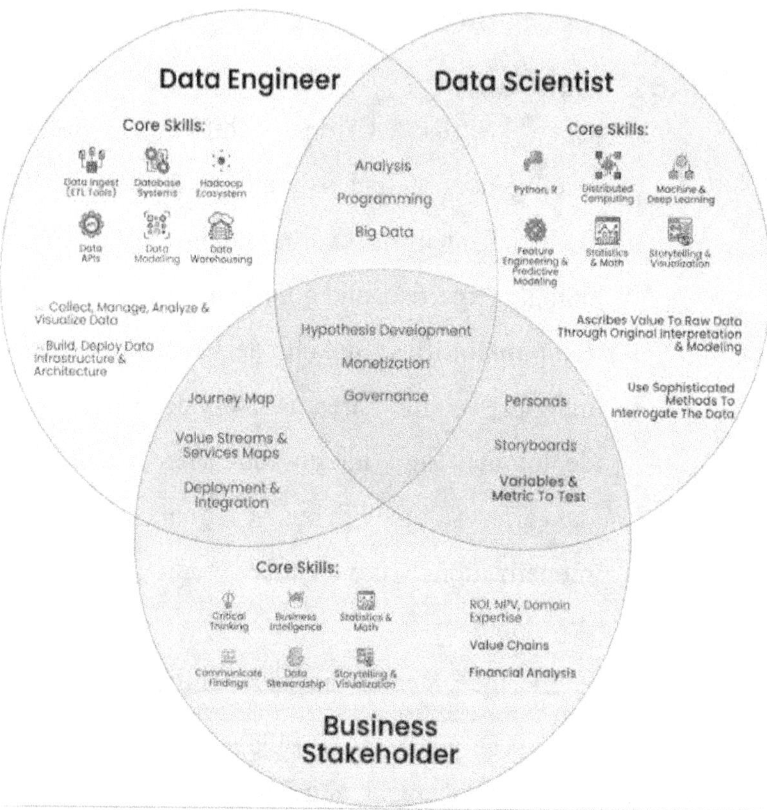


## 1.6 DevOps Vs DataOps vs. MLOps

# DevOps

- **Focus:** Software development and IT operations.

- **Objective:** Streamlining and automating the software development lifecycle (SDLC) to deliver applications and services rapidly and reliably. DevOps emphasizes collaboration between development and operations teams through practices like Continuous Integration and Continuous Deployment (CI/CD).

## DataOps

- **Focus:** Data management and analytics.
- **Objective:** Enhancing the efficiency and reliability of data pipelines and analytics processes. DataOps applies DevOps principles to data workflows, ensuring data quality, governance, and faster delivery of insights. It facilitates collaboration between data engineers, data scientists, and analysts to create a more agile and data-driven culture.

## MLOps

- **Focus:** Machine learning (ML) models and AI systems.
- **Objective:** Managing the lifecycle of ML models from development to deployment and monitoring. MLOps integrates practices from DevOps and DataOps to handle the unique challenges of deploying and maintaining machine learning models, such as versioning, scalability, and continuous improvement based on new data.

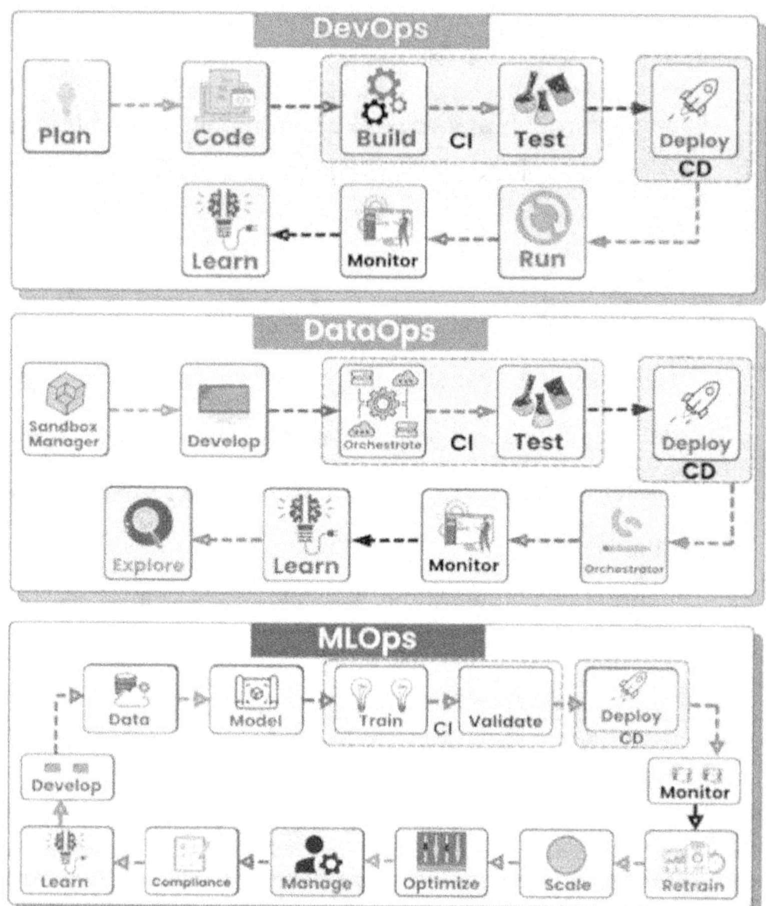


Each of these methodologies addresses specific organizational needs, with DevOps focusing on software, DataOps on data, and MLOps on machine learning, contributing to more efficient, reliable, and scalable operations.

## 1.7 Foundational Knowledge for Data Science

***Step 1***: **Establish Your Basis**

- **Mathematical:** Review statistics, calculus, and linear algebra.
- **Programming:** As they are necessary for machine learning, learn Python or R.
- **Data Handling:** Learn how to use libraries for data manipulation like NumPy and Pandas.

### *Step 2*: **Comprehend the Principles of Machine Learning**

- **First**: what is machine learning? Discover the principles of machine learning and its various forms, including reinforcement, unsupervised, and supervised learning.
- **Algorithms**: Examine fundamental algorithms like decision trees, clustering methods, and linear regression.

### *Step 3:* **Investigate Courses and Resources**

- **Online Courses:** To locate structured learning pathways, use resources on GitHub or sites such as Coursera, DataCamp, or free courses.
- **Books and Articles:** To expand your knowledge, read books and articles that have been recommended.

### *Step 4:* **Real-World Implementation** 

- **Projects:** To put what you've learned into practice, start with simple tasks like classifying photos or estimating home prices.
- **Kaggle Competitions:** Take part in Kaggle challenges to hone your skills and obtain practical experience.

***Step 5:*** **Join the Community**

- **Networking:** To connect with other students and professionals, and participate in local gatherings, forums, and online communities.
- **Mentorship:** Look for mentors who can help you as you pursue your education.

Remain interested, accept the obstacles, and never forget that practice makes perfect.

## 1.8 Data Science's Most Important Skills

| Skill | Description |
|---|---|
| Programming Languages | Python, R, SQL |
| Data Manipulation and Cleaning | Pandas, dplyr, tidyverse, polars |
| Statistical Analysis | Descriptive statistics, Hypothesis testing, Probability, Distributions |
| Data Visualization | Matplotlib, Seaborn, ggplot2, Plotly |

# Data Scientist Roadmap

| Skill | Description |
| --- | --- |
| Machine Learning Algorithms - Supervised Learning | Linear Regression, Logistic Regression, Decision Trees, Random Forests, SVM, GBM, XGBoost |
| Machine Learning Algorithms - Unsupervised Learning | K-Means Clustering, PCA, UMAP |
| Deep Learning | Neural Networks, CNNs, RNNs, LSTM |
| Natural Language Processing (NLP) | Tokenization, stemming/lemmatization, TF-IDF, Word Embeddings, Transformers (BERT, GPT) |
| Generative AI | LLMs, RAG, AI Agents, Agent Workflows, Supervision, Plan and Execute, LangChain, LangGraph |
| Time Series Analysis | ARIMA, SARIMA, Machine Learning for Time Series, Nixlta in Python, Modetime in R |
| Big Data Technologies | Spark, Polars |
| Model Deployment and Production | Streamlit, Shiny, Docker, DockerHub |
| Database Management | PostgreSQL, MySQL |
| Version Control | Git, GitHub |
| Cloud Computing | AWS, Azure, Google Cloud Platform (GCP) |
| Optimization Techniques | scipy.optimize, pyomo, R Optimization Infrastructure (ROI) |
| Business Acumen and Communication | Translating data insights into business strategy, Effective communication skills, and Soft skills |

# Chapter 2

# Statistics and Mathematics

## 2.1  Mathematics

### 2.1.1  Linear Algebra

Linear Algebra is the most important piece of mathematics that every data scientist should know. Machine learning and deep learning concepts use this topic extensively.

Machine learning involves programming computers to learn from data instead of relying on predefined instructions. It uses math to help machines find the best solution, a process known as model training. The foundation of this process is linear algebra, which provides the tools for representing data and computations in machine learning models. Linear algebra focuses on arrays, including vectors, matrices, and tensors, which are essential for handling data in ML.

In mathematics, linear equations and their matrices-based vector space representation are the subject of linear algebra. This is the foundation of data science and is particularly crucial for machine learning, as most machine learning models can be represented as matrices. Linear algebra is used in model validation, data transformation, and data preprocessing.

This addresses a fundamental issue with data representation

and computation in machine learning models: you can easily represent and compute over a given dataset using linear algebra, which in turn solves your business challenge.

The scalar, vector, matrix, and tensor are the fundamental elements of linear algebra.

_scalar:_ a single number

_vector:_ a one-dimensional array of numbers

_matrix:_ a two-dimensional array of numbers

_tensor:_ a multi-dimensional array of numbers

| Scalar | Vector | Matrix | Tensor |
|---|---|---|---|
| scalar = 1 | np.array([1,2]) | np.array( [1,1],[2,2] ) | np.array( [1,1],[2,2], [3,3],[4,4] ) |

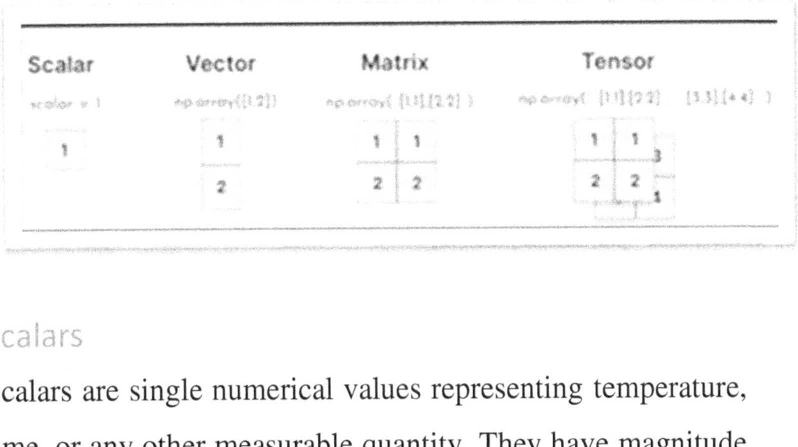

## Scalars

Scalars are single numerical values representing temperature, time, or any other measurable quantity. They have magnitude but no direction. Examples of scalars include temperatures like 30 degrees Celsius or time intervals like 5 seconds.

There are various sets of numbers of interest within machine learning. N represents the set of positive integers (1,2,3,…). Z represents the integers, which include positive, negative, and zero values. Q represents the set of *rational* numbers that may be expressed as a fraction of two integers.

## Vectors

Both magnitude and direction are components of vectors. Number arrays are used to represent vectors in the linear algebra setting. The vectors can be described as arrows in space, with the direction denoting the orientation and the length signifying the magnitude of the vector. Physical quantities like force, position, and velocity are frequently represented as vectors. Vectors can, for instance, be used to describe an object's position in three dimensions or the speed of a moving automobile.

In machine learning vectors often represent *feature vectors*, with their individual components specifying how important a particular feature is. Such features could include the relative importance of words in a text document, the intensity of a set of pixels in a two-dimensional image, or historical price values for a cross-section of financial instruments.

## Matrices

Matrices are among the most crucial mathematical subjects in Linear Algebra. Matrix applications are not simply for solving mathematical puzzles; they are also used in a wide range of fields, including wireless communication, data science, machine learning, cryptography, and many more. We will talk about many matrix types in this article along with some examples. We will also go over a few unique matrices, like the orthogonal matrix, involutory matrix, and idempotent matrix, in the last part.

In deep learning neural network weights are stored as matrices, while feature inputs are stored as vectors. Formulating the problem in terms of linear algebra allows compact handling of these computations.

A matrix is a rectangular arrangement of data in rows and columns to form an array.

- The **horizontal** arrangement is called: **a row**
- The **vertical** arrangement is called: a **column.**

*Notation*: Any matrix having *m* rows and *n* columns is given by: $[A]_{m \times n}$.

$$[A]_{m \times n} = \begin{bmatrix} a_{11} & a_{12} & a_{13} & a_{14} & \cdots & \cdots & \cdots & a_{1n} \\ a_{21} & a_{22} & a_{23} & a_{24} & \cdots & \cdots & \cdots & a_{2n} \\ a_{31} & a_{32} & a_{33} & a_{34} & \cdots & \cdots & \cdots & a_{3n} \\ \cdots & \cdots & \cdots & \cdots & \cdots & \cdots & \cdots & \cdots \\ \cdots & \cdots & \cdots & \cdots & \cdots & \cdots & \cdots & \cdots \\ \cdots & \cdots & \cdots & \cdots & \cdots & \cdots & \cdots & \cdots \\ a_{m1} & a_{m2} & a_{m3} & a_{m4} & \cdots & \cdots & \cdots & a_{mn} \end{bmatrix}$$

## The different types of matrices

- **Singleton Matrix**: Contains only one element. Example: [1], [0], [9].

- **Row Matrix**: Has only one row, with any number of columns. Example: [1, 2, 3].

- **Column Matrix**: Has only one column, with any number of rows.

- **Null/Zero Matrix**: All elements are zero. It can be square or rectangular.

- **Square Matrix**: Has the same number of rows and columns. Example: A 2x2 matrix.

- **Diagonal Matrix**: A square matrix where all non-diagonal elements are zero, and diagonal elements can be non-zero. Example: [1, 0; 0, 2].

- **Scalar Matrix**: A diagonal matrix with all diagonal elements being equal.

- **Identity Matrix**: A special case of a scalar matrix where diagonal elements are 1.

- **Triangular Matrix**: A square matrix where either all elements above or below the principal diagonal are zero. Two types:

    - **Upper Triangular**: Zeroes below the diagonal.

    - **Lower Triangular**: Zeroes above the diagonal.

- **Symmetric Matrix**: A square matrix equal to its transpose. Example: $A = A^T$.

- **Skew-Symmetric Matrix**: A square matrix where $A = -A^T$.

- **Idempotent Matrix**: A square matrix where $A^2 = A$.

- **Involutory Matrix**: A square matrix where $A^2 = I$ (identity matrix).

- **Orthogonal Matrix**: A square matrix where $A.A^T = I$ (identity matrix).

## Applications of Linear Algebra in Machine Learning

- **Solving Linear Equation Systems**: Linear algebra helps solve systems of linear equations by representing them as matrices and vectors. Instead of using traditional methods that require iterative element elimination, matrix operations (like taking the inverse of a matrix) solve variables more efficiently. This process, which may seem trivial for small systems, greatly improves computational efficiency in machine learning models.

$$\begin{bmatrix} 3 & 2 \\ 1 & -1 \end{bmatrix} \cdot \begin{bmatrix} a \\ b \end{bmatrix} = \begin{bmatrix} 7 \\ -1 \end{bmatrix}$$

- **Linear Regression**: Linear algebra generalizes well to linear regression models. Instead of using loops to compute weighted sums for individual instances, matrix representation allows for faster computation by optimizing the coefficient vector through linear operations. Libraries like Numpy and Pandas use vectorization to speed up this process, avoiding time-consuming loops.

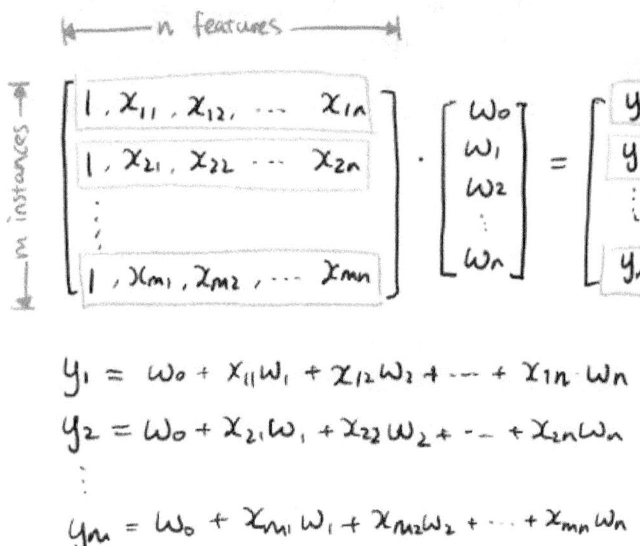

$$y_1 = W_0 + X_{11}W_1 + X_{12}W_2 + \cdots + X_{1n}W_n$$
$$y_2 = W_0 + X_{21}W_1 + X_{22}W_2 + \cdots + X_{2n}W_n$$
$$\vdots$$
$$y_m = W_0 + X_{m1}W_1 + X_{m2}W_2 + \cdots + X_{mn}W_n$$

**Neural Networks**: In neural networks, linear algebra is used to model the interconnected layers of nodes. Each node's output is weighted and aggregated to form inputs for the next layer. This process, resembling linear regression, scales up to large datasets by using matrices to store weights. In deep learning, tensors (multi-dimensional arrays) are used to handle complex data structures, such as the RGB channels in images processed by Convolutional Neural Networks (CNNs).

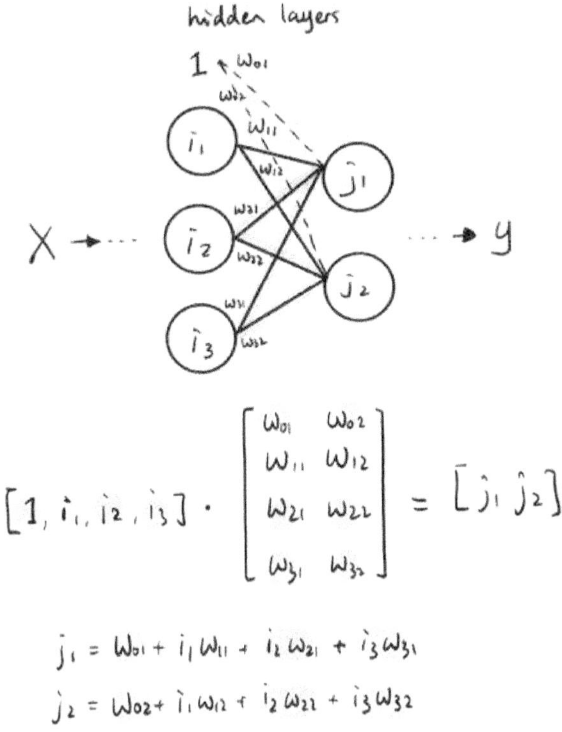



$$[1, i_1, i_2, i_3] \cdot \begin{bmatrix} W_{01} & W_{02} \\ W_{11} & W_{12} \\ W_{21} & W_{22} \\ W_{31} & W_{32} \end{bmatrix} = [j_1 \; j_2]$$

$$j_1 = W_{01} + i_1 W_{11} + i_2 W_{21} + i_3 W_{31}$$

$$j_2 = W_{02} + i_1 W_{12} + i_2 W_{21} + i_3 W_{32}$$

***Real-world use case:*** The learning algorithms need numbers to work on. Data such as images have to be converted to an array of numbers before the data is fed to the algorithms. An image of 50*50 is first converted to a 50*50 matrix. Thus, the value of a pixel ranges from 0 to 255. The resulting image is then converted to a vector of dimension 2500. This way an image is converted to a vector.

## Tensors

Tensors extend the idea of matrices and vectors to greater dimensions. In contrast, tensors can have any number of dimensions, matrices are two-dimensional, vectors are one-dimensional, and scalars are zero-dimensional. Tensors are frequently used to represent multi-dimensional data, including time series data, volumetric data, and color images.

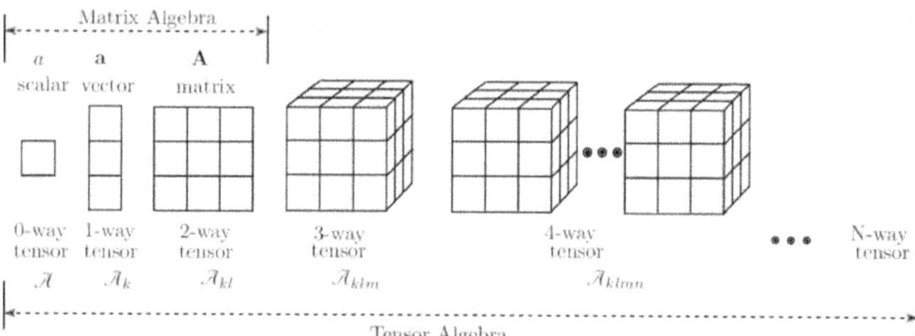


Working with color images and video data will involve tensors. The dimensions of a color image will be something like height, breadth, and color axis when it is transformed into an array of numbers. For Red, Green, and Blue channels, the color axis essentially defines a new set of numbers. We will be building a matrix based on the pixel value for every color channel. After that, a vector is formed by unrolling the generated matrices.

## 2.1.2  Calculus

Calculus is a branch of mathematics that deals with calculating instantaneous rates of change (differential calculus) and the summation of infinitely small factors to determine a whole (integral calculus). It is essential for understanding concepts like velocity, slopes, and the area under a curve.

In data science and machine learning, calculus is vital for optimizing models. Ever wonder how logistic regression or gradient descent algorithms work? To grasp their implementation, you need to understand key concepts like limits, continuity, differentiation, integration, and multivariate calculus. These concepts reveal the mechanics behind the algorithms.

Calculus has two major subfields:

- **Differential Calculus:** This branch focuses on the rate of change between quantities. Its primary goal is to identify the minima and maxima of functions, which helps in finding optimal solutions. Topics in differential calculus include:
  - Functions, Domains, Ranges, Dependent and Independent Variables
  - Limits and Continuity
  - Derivatives & Partial Derivatives
    - ✓ Taylor Series
    - ✓ Directional Derivatives
    - ✓ Higher Order Derivatives
- **Integral Calculus:** This branch deals with finding the total size or value, such as lengths, areas, and volumes. It uses integration (anti-derivatives) to compute these

measurements, focusing on understanding integration formulas and their implementation.

Using a training dataset, a machine learning algorithm such as classification regression or clustering determines weight factors that may be applied to unknown data to make predictions. Every machine learning model has an optimization algorithm that primarily uses calculus.

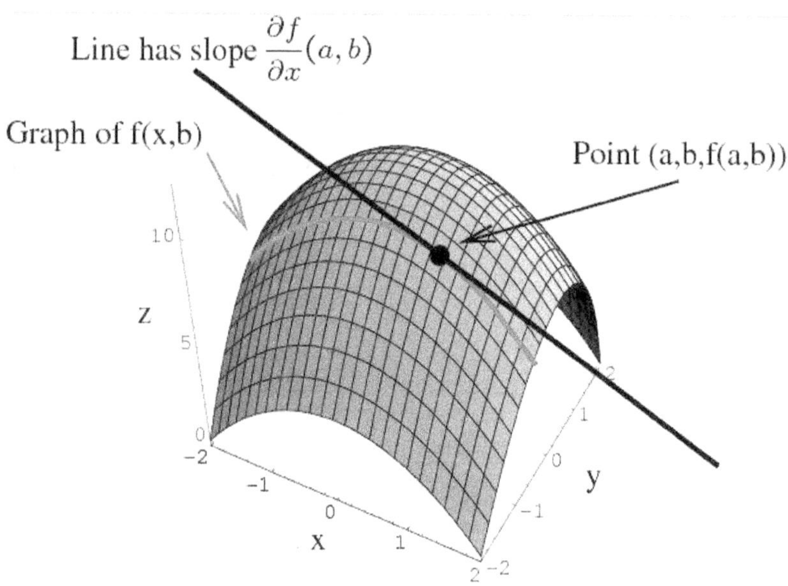


A dataset containing several characteristics or predictors is used to build most machine learning models. Therefore, having a solid understanding of multivariable calculus is crucial for developing a machine learning model.

***The following are the subjects you should know about:***

*Functions of several variables; Derivatives and gradients;*

*Step function, Sigmoid function, Logit function, ReLU (Rectified Linear Unit) function; Cost function; Plotting of functions; Minimum and Maximum values of a function.*

## The Three Essential Areas of Calculus for Machine Learning

### ❑ Differentiation

Differentiation is a fundamental concept in calculus, describing how a function changes as its inputs change. In machine learning, it's essential to understand how tuning parameters affect model behavior. Differentiation allows us to compute gradients, which indicate the direction and rate of change of a function. Whether you're optimizing a cost function in a neural network or analyzing how input features influence predictions, differentiation is the cornerstone of these operations.

Almost every machine learning algorithm from gradient descent to backpropagation relies on differentiation. Mastering the notations, such as partial derivatives and chain rule, will enable you to grasp how algorithms update their parameters to improve model performance.

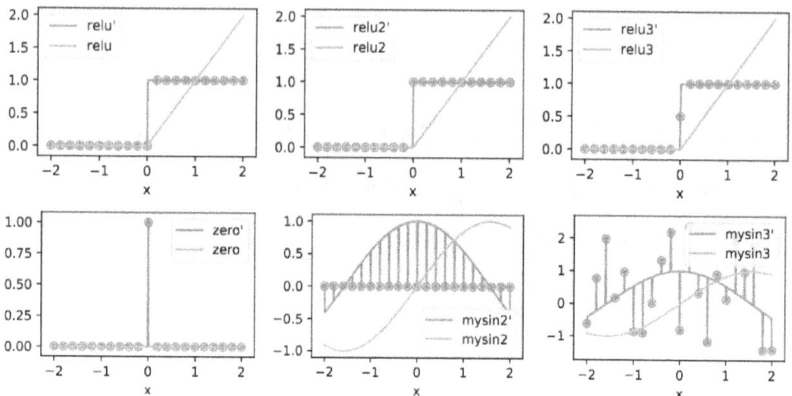

The previous Figure shows two distinct implementations of the same function and automatic differentiation applied to relu is shown at the top. at the bottom, the sine function's arbitrary derivatives at specified parameters, artificial critical point generation, and automatic differentiation of a constant function.

## ❑ Vector Calculus

Vector calculus extends differentiation into higher dimensions, which is critical because most machine learning models involve multiple inputs (features) and often multiple outputs (predictions). Understanding multivariate calculus allows you to work with vector-valued functions, which are used to describe the behavior of algorithms with multiple variables.

For example, in neural networks, we deal with gradients that are vectors or matrices representing how each weight influences the loss function. This is the foundation of backpropagation, the algorithm used to train neural networks.

Knowing how to compute and represent derivatives in vector or matrix form is crucial to understanding and implementing these models effectively.

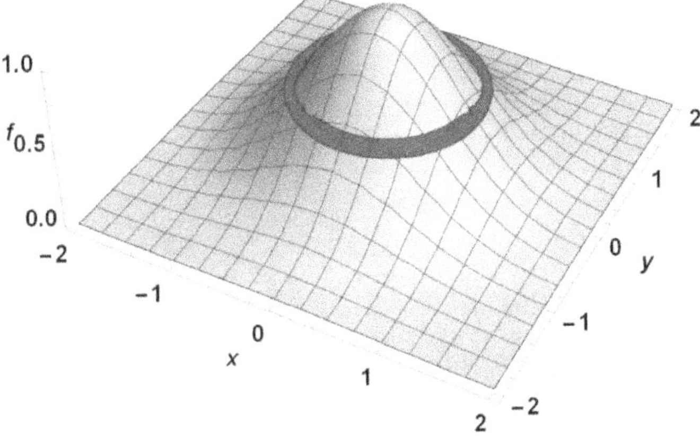

## ❑ Calculus for Optimization

One of the most powerful applications of calculus in machine learning is optimization. Differentiation helps us find the optimal values of parameters whether we're maximizing or minimizing a function. In many machine learning models, we seek to minimize a loss function, which measures how well the model performs. Through calculus, we can determine the function's minima or maxima efficiently.

For example, the support vector machine (SVM) classifier is essentially an optimization problem, where the goal is to find the maximum margin that separates two classes. Understanding how calculus works in constrained optimization allows you to grasp how SVM finds this solution, or how Lagrange multipliers are used in optimization problems with constraints.

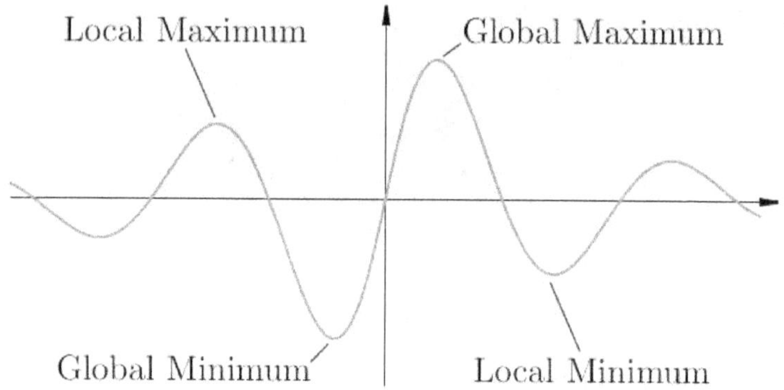


## 2.1.3   Information Theory

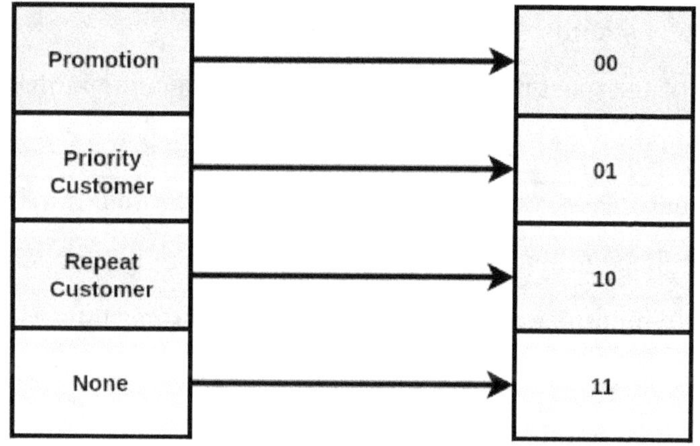


Information can be represented as bits, with each bit allowing a choice between two equally probable alternatives. For 'n' sequential choices, with 'm' final outcomes, m = 2^n, or n=log2(m). Information is essentially a mathematical representation of uncertainty.

When transmitting data over a communication channel, there is often a probability 'p' of error, where the received message may differ from the transmitted one. While physical changes to the communication system can reduce errors, they are often costly. Instead, information theory and coding theory provide solutions to improve error detection and correction using encoders and decoders. These theoretical frameworks help create reliable channels without physical alterations, simply by improving how information is processed.

Key Concepts:

- **_Channel Capacity:_** The maximum information that can be transmitted through a channel.
- **_Data Compression (Source Coding):_** More frequent events should have shorter encodings.
- **_Error Correction (Channel Coding):_** Methods to detect and correct errors introduced by noise in the channel.

Information theory plays a critical role in machine learning and data analytics by helping measure and improve the accuracy of data used for building predictive models.

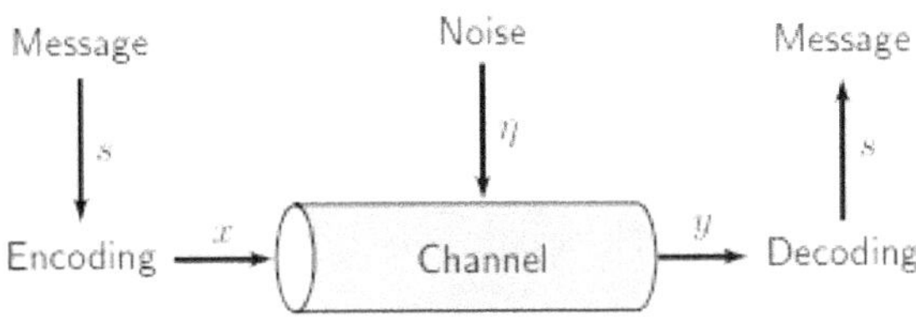

## 2.1.4  Numerical Analysis

A key component of machine learning is numerical analysis, which deals with creating and using algorithms to solve ongoing mathematical problems. Given that machine learning frequently entails managing big datasets and carrying out intricate computations, numerical analysis offers the mathematical underpinnings necessary to guarantee the accuracy and efficiency of these operations.

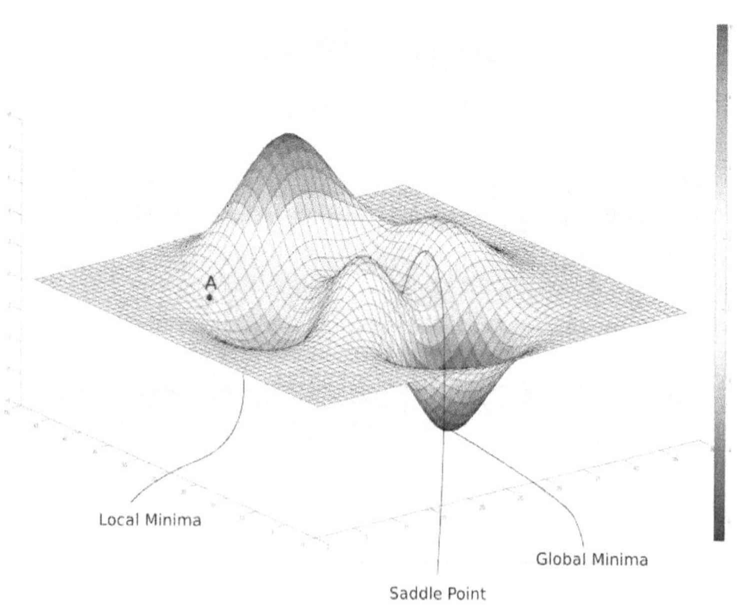


There are numerous ways in which machine learning incorporates numerical analysis:

## Optimization Algorithms

Machine learning relies heavily on optimization, particularly while training models. Numerical optimization techniques include algorithms like Newton's method, gradient descent, and their variations. These methods update the model parameters iteratively to minimize or maximize a cost function. Finding the parameters that reduce the error between the expected and actual values is the aim.

- ***Gradient Descent:*** A popular optimization algorithm that uses numerical differentiation to update model weights by calculating the gradient of the cost function. It requires careful tuning of the learning rate and is subject to issues like vanishing or exploding gradients.

- ***Newton's Method:*** A more advanced optimization technique that uses second-order derivatives (Hessian matrices) to update parameters. While it converges faster, it's computationally expensive for large datasets.

## Matrix Computations

Many machine learning models, especially those used in deep learning, rely heavily on matrix and vector computations. Linear algebra operations like matrix multiplication, inversion, and decomposition are fundamental, and efficient numerical algorithms are required to handle these operations, especially when working with high-dimensional data.

- ***Principal Component Analysis (PCA):*** These dimensionality reduction techniques are based on numerical methods that decompose large matrices into simpler components, helping reduce the computational complexity of models.

- ***Cholesky Decomposition:*** Used in algorithms like Gaussian Processes for making matrix inversion more efficient, especially for large covariance matrices.

## Numerical Stability

Ensuring numerical stability is crucial in machine learning, as algorithms that are not numerically stable may result in significant errors or crashes, especially with large datasets or high-dimensional spaces. Numerical precision issues can arise from operations like matrix inversion or differentiation, causing loss of significant digits or overflow.

For example, regularization techniques like L2 regularization (Ridge Regression) are often used to control the size of parameters and prevent overfitting. From a numerical perspective, regularization also stabilizes the solution by preventing extreme values during optimization.

## Numerical Differentiation

Machine learning models often rely on gradient-based optimization. In such cases, numerical differentiation techniques such as finite differences or automatic differentiation are used to compute gradients of the loss function concerning model parameters. These methods are critical in backpropagation for training neural networks.

- ***Finite Differences:*** Approximates derivatives by evaluating the function at nearby points. It's easy to implement but can be less accurate for very small step sizes and can introduce errors due to rounding.

- ***Automatic Differentiation:*** Used in modern machine learning frameworks (e.g., TensorFlow, PyTorch), this technique computes exact derivatives programmatically without human intervention, improving efficiency and accuracy.

## Linear and Non-Linear Systems of Equations

In machine learning, solving systems of equations is often required, particularly in algorithms like linear regression or support vector machines. Numerical methods for solving these systems include:

- ***LU Decomposition:*** Decomposes a matrix into lower and upper triangular matrices for more efficient solving of linear systems.

- ***Iterative Methods:*** Such as Gauss-Seidel or Conjugate Gradient, are used when dealing with large-scale systems of equations that are too complex for direct methods.

## Stochastic Methods

Many machine learning algorithms rely on stochastic methods, especially when handling large datasets or dealing with non-deterministic processes. Monte Carlo methods are a prime example, where numerical simulations and random sampling are used to estimate solutions to complex problems, such as evaluating the posterior distribution in Bayesian models.

## Handling High-Dimensional Data

Numerical analysis is essential when working with high-dimensional data, where the "curse of dimensionality" becomes an issue. Efficient numerical methods help reduce computation time and memory usage. Techniques like gradient-based optimization (for large parameter spaces) and kernel methods (for non-linear data) leverage numerical analysis to efficiently process high-dimensional data.

## Error Approximation and Convergence

Numerical methods often involve approximation, and understanding the error in these approximations is critical.

Machine learning models also rely on iterative algorithms that converge to a solution, so ensuring fast and accurate convergence is a major focus of numerical analysis. Error bounds and convergence rates help practitioners understand how close their solution is to the true value and how quickly they can reach it.

The computational tools that form the foundation of many machine learning methods are provided by numerical analysis. Numerical analysis guarantees that machine learning models are both accurate and efficient, allowing them to scale to real-world applications. This includes both optimization and matrix calculations, as well as numerical stability and stochastic approaches. Gaining an understanding of these ideas might improve one's capacity to create machine-learning models that are more reliable, particularly in situations requiring huge datasets or intricate calculations.

## 2.1.5  Graph Theory

Graph theory, which is the study of networks or graphs, is becoming more and more important in machine learning and data science. A graph is a useful abstraction for expressing intricate relationships in data. It comprises nodes, also known as vertices, and edges, or connections between nodes. Graph theory is used in many fields of machine learning, including natural language processing, recommendation systems, network analysis, and social network modeling.

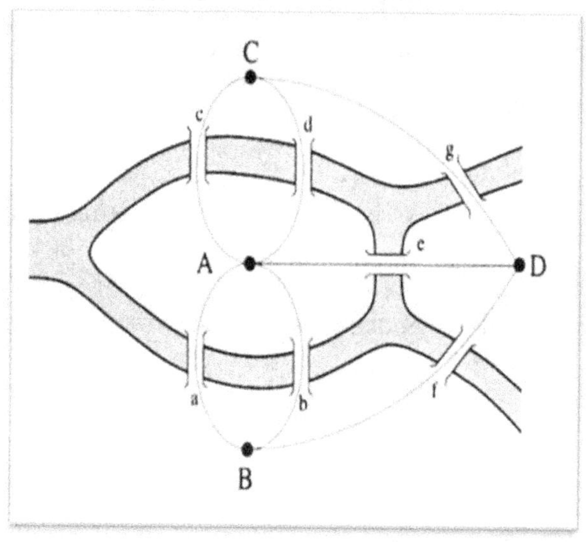

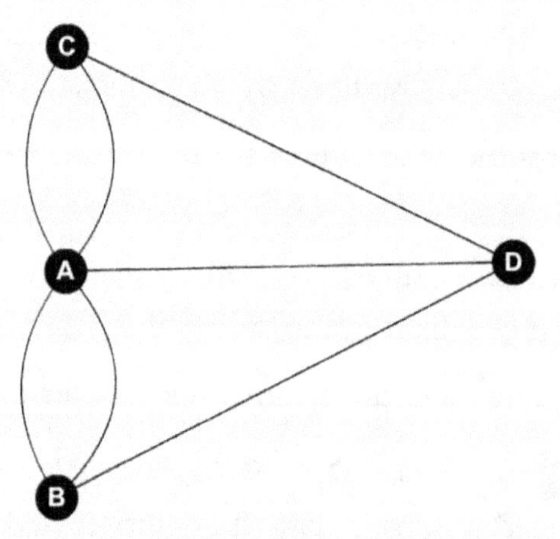

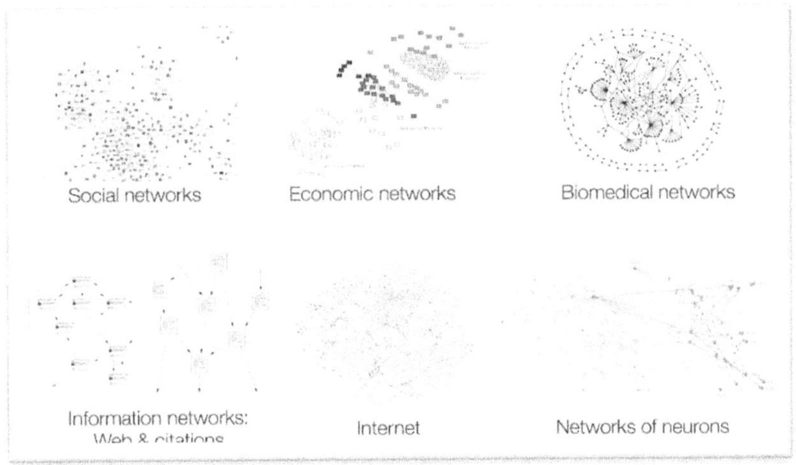



## Graph Representation of Data

Graphs provide a natural way to represent and analyze relationships between data points. In many real-world applications, data is inherently structured as graphs:

- ***Social Networks:*** In a social network, nodes represent users, and edges represent relationships (e.g., friendships or followers).

- ***Knowledge Graphs:*** These represent relationships between entities (people, places, things) in a way that captures the semantic meaning between them. Knowledge graphs are used by companies like Google to enhance search results by understanding connections between concepts.

- ***Recommendation Systems:*** In collaborative filtering,

users and items can be represented as nodes, and an edge between a user and an item might indicate a user's interaction or preference, forming a bipartite graph.

- ***Molecular Structures:*** In chemistry and biology, molecular structures can be represented as graphs, where atoms are nodes, and chemical bonds are edges. Machine learning models can use this representation to predict molecular properties or interactions.

## Graph-Based Algorithms

Many algorithms in machine learning and data science are based on graph theory principles, used to extract insights or solve optimization problems on graph structures.

- ***PageRank***: Developed by Google, PageRank is a graph-based algorithm used to rank the importance of nodes (web pages) in a graph based on the structure of incoming and outgoing links.

- ***Shortest Path Algorithms:*** Algorithms like **Dijkstra's** and **Bellman-Ford** are used to find the shortest path between nodes in a graph. These are important in routing problems, recommendation systems, and decision-making tasks.

- ***Minimum Spanning Tree (MST):*** MST algorithms, such as **Kruskal's** and **Prim's**, are used to find a tree that spans all nodes in a graph with the minimum sum of edge weights. MSTs are useful in clustering and network design problems.

- ***Community Detection:*** Algorithms such as **Louvain** and **Girvan-Newman** help find groups of closely connected nodes, or communities, within a larger network. Community detection is used in social network analysis and recommendation systems.

## Graph Neural Networks (GNNs)

Graph Neural Networks (GNNs) are a class of machine learning algorithms designed to handle graph-structured data. GNNs have gained popularity for their ability to capture complex relationships and dependencies between nodes in a graph.

- ***Node Classification:*** GNNs can be used to predict the label of a node based on its features and the features of neighboring nodes. For example, in social network analysis, GNNs might classify users based on their connections and activities.

- ***Link Prediction:*** GNNs are used to predict missing links between nodes, which is useful for applications like recommendation systems (predicting new friendships or interactions) or knowledge graph completion.

- ***Graph Classification:*** GNNs can be applied to classify entire graphs. For example, in drug discovery, GNNs can predict whether a molecule (represented as a graph) has certain properties or biological activities.

## Spectral Graph Theory

Spectral graph theory applies the concepts of linear algebra to graphs, focusing on the eigenvalues and eigenvectors of matrices associated with graphs (e.g., adjacency matrix or Laplacian matrix). It is used to understand the structure and properties of graphs and is particularly relevant in machine learning for tasks such as dimensionality reduction and clustering.

- ***Graph Laplacian:*** This matrix is central in spectral graph theory and is used in algorithms like **spectral clustering**, which finds clusters by analyzing the eigenvalues of the graph Laplacian. Spectral clustering is popular in scenarios where data points are not easily separable in their original space.

- ***Graph Embeddings***: By projecting a graph into a lower-dimensional space using techniques from spectral graph theory, it becomes easier to apply traditional machine learning algorithms. Graph embeddings help capture relationships between nodes in a continuous space, allowing for efficient learning of node or edge features.

## Network Analysis and Centrality Measures

In data science, graph theory is often used to analyze networks by measuring the importance or centrality of nodes and edges within a graph.

- ***Degree Centrality:*** Measures the number of connections a node has. It's a simple metric but important in understanding how connected a node is within a graph. In social networks, this could represent how popular a user is.

- ***Betweenness Centrality:*** Measures the number of times a node acts as a bridge along the shortest path between two other nodes. Nodes with high betweenness centrality often control the flow of information in a network.

- ***Eigenvector Centrality:*** Similar to Google's PageRank, this measure considers not only the number of connections a node has but also the importance of those connections. Nodes connected to other high-importance nodes will have higher eigenvector centrality.

## Graph-Based Clustering

Graph theory provides useful techniques for clustering data points based on their relationships. One of the main techniques is **graph partitioning**, where the graph is divided into subgraphs or clusters that share dense internal connections while having sparse external connections.

- ***Spectral Clustering:*** Uses the spectrum (eigenvalues) of the Laplacian matrix of a graph to perform dimensionality reduction before clustering data points. This is especially useful when the data is non-linearly separable in its original form.

- ***Community Detection:*** This clustering technique finds groups of nodes that are densely connected within a graph, often revealing insights into social networks, biological systems, and more.

## Graph-Based Reinforcement Learning

In reinforcement learning, graph theory can be used to represent environments, states, and actions. For example, in **Markov Decision Processes (MDPs)**, states are represented as nodes, and transitions between states are edges. Agents navigate this graph by taking actions (traversing edges) to maximize cumulative rewards.

- ***Graph-Structured Environments:*** In some applications, like robotics or game AI, environments can be represented as graphs, and graph theory helps in modeling decision-making processes.

Graph theory provides essential tools for analyzing and understanding complex relationships in data. Whether it's through advanced graph algorithms, graph neural networks, or spectral methods, graph theory enhances the ability of data scientists and machine learning practitioners to model, analyze, and extract meaningful insights from structured data. As the amount of interconnected data continues to grow, graph theory's relevance in data science and machine learning is only set to increase.

## 2.2 Probabilities and Statistics

Probability and statistics are fundamental to data science, providing the theoretical framework for making inferences from data. **Probability** helps model uncertainty, allowing data scientists to predict outcomes and assess risks in decision-making. It is essential in building machine learning models, where concepts like conditional probability, Bayes' theorem, and distributions guide predictive analytics. **Statistics**, on the other hand, enables data scientists to collect, analyze, and interpret data. Techniques like hypothesis testing, regression analysis, and variance measurement help conclude data, uncover patterns, and validate model performance. Together, probability and statistics form the backbone of data-driven decisions in data science.

## 2.2.1  Descriptive Statistics

Descriptive statistics describe the essential characteristics of your data. Using measures of central tendency, like mean, median, mode, and dispersion, we can measure range, standard deviation, variance, etc. Data can be summarized using charts, tables, and graphs.

Brief informational coefficients known as descriptive statistics are used to provide an overview of a specific data collection, which may be a sample or a representative of the full population. measurements of central tendency and measurements of variability (spread) are the two categories into which descriptive statistics fall. The standard deviation, variance, minimum and maximum variables, kurtosis, and skewness are measurements of variability, whereas the mean, median, and mode are measures of central tendency.

## Types of Descriptive Statistics

- **Central Tendency:** This focuses on the central values of a data set, using the mean, median, or mode to describe the center position of a distribution. These measures help summarize the most common patterns in the data.

- **Measures of Variability:** These describe the spread or dispersion within a data set. They go beyond averages to indicate how data points are distributed. Common measures include range, quartiles, absolute deviation, and variance.

- **Distribution:** Distribution, or frequency distribution, refers to how often each data point occurs within a data set. For instance, it categorizes the frequency of specific values or groups, such as gender classifications.

## Descriptive Statistics and Outliers

Outliers are data points that significantly deviate from the rest of the dataset and can be errors, anomalies, or rare events. In descriptive statistics, identifying and managing outliers is crucial for accurate data analysis. Graphical techniques (e.g., boxplots) and statistical methods (e.g., Z-scores, IQR) help detect outliers.

Outliers can skew descriptive statistics, especially measures of central tendency like the mean, which can be disproportionately influenced by extreme values. For example, a dataset of (1, 1, 1, 997) results in a mean of 250, which is misleading. Depending on the situation, outliers can be removed if irrelevant or kept if they provide valuable insight. Their relevance should be carefully considered when performing descriptive statistics.

## 2.2.2   Inferential statistics

Inferential statistics aim to conclude a sample and generalize them to the population. It is about using data from a sample and then making inferences about the larger population from which it is drawn.

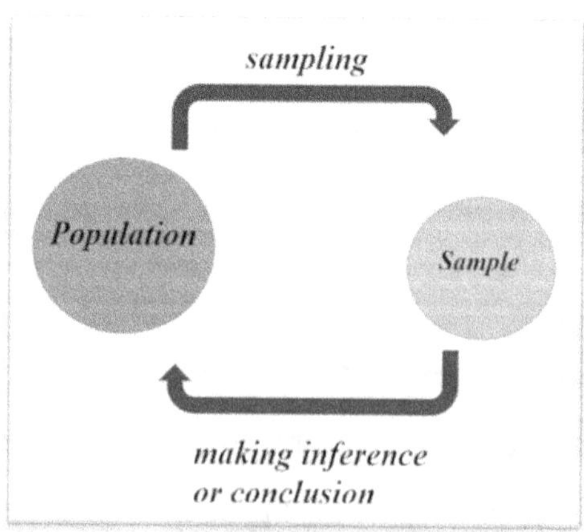

The most common methodologies used are hypothesis testing and analysis of variance:

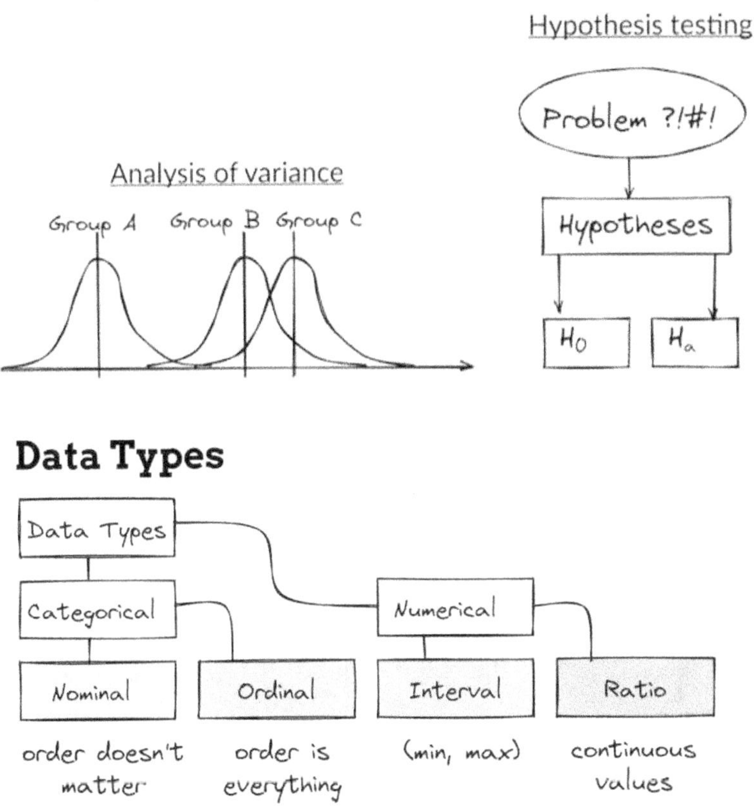


## Data Types



Descriptive statistics vs. Inferential statistics

Descriptive statistics summarize past data, providing insights such as sales counts, average quantities, and daily sales trends. These statistics simply describe what has already occurred without going beyond the given information. On the other hand, inferential statistics take this summarized data and apply it to make predictions or decisions about another set, such as forecasting sales for a new product based on past sales trends. Descriptive statistics describe past events, while inferential statistics use that data to predict future outcomes or apply it to different scenarios.

## 2.2.3   Central Limit Theorem

A statistical theory known as the central limit theorem (CLT) states that, for a population with a limited degree of variance, if a sufficiently enough sample size is taken, the mean of all samples taken from that population will resemble the overall mean.

Stated differently, the shape of the mean distribution that results from repeatedly taking samples from a given population is precisely what the central limit theorem describes. In particular, the distribution of means derived from repeated sampling will converge to normalcy as sample sizes increase.

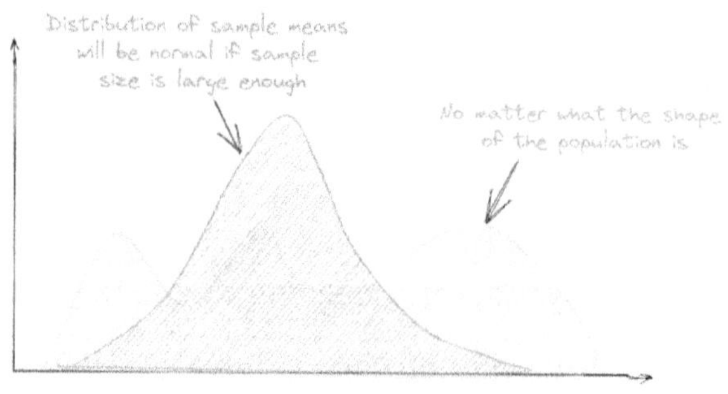

## Central Limit Theorem Definition

*Central limit theorem (CLT) is a statistical theory given that as sample sizes get larger, the mean of all samples will be approximately equal to the mean of the mean of the mean of the population, and the distribution of means will approach normality.*

## Components of the Central Limit Theorem

As the sample size increases, the sampling distribution of the mean, X-bar, can be approximated by a normal distribution with mean $\mu$ and <u>standard deviation</u> $\sigma/\sqrt{n}$ where:

- *$\mu$ is the population mean*
- *$\sigma$ is the population standard deviation*
- *$n$ is the sample size*

In other words, if we repeatedly take independent, random samples of size n from any population, then when n is large, the sample means will approach a normal distribution.

The Central Limit Theorem states that for large sample sizes ($n \geq 30$), the distribution of sample means will approximate a normal distribution, even if the population distribution is not normal. When random samples are taken from a population with mean $\mu$ and standard deviation $\sigma$, the sample means will tend to be normally distributed as the sample size increases.

A sample size of 30 is typically large enough to demonstrate this effect. If the population distribution is close to normal, fewer samples are required. However, if the population is highly skewed, a larger number of samples is needed to observe the Central Limit Theorem in action.

The Central Limit Theorem (CLT) primarily deals with the distribution of sample means, and there are two key equations related to CLT:

- ***Mean of the Sampling Distribution ($\mu\bar{x}$):***

The mean of the sampling distribution of the sample means ($\mu\bar{x}$) is equal to the mean of the population ($\mu$):

$$\mu\bar{x} = \mu$$

This indicates that the average of the sample means will converge to the population mean as the sample size increases.

- ***Standard Deviation of the Sampling Distribution ($\sigma\bar{x}$):***

The standard deviation of the sampling distribution of the sample means (also known as the standard error of the mean, $\sigma\bar{x}$) is equal to the population standard deviation ($\sigma$) divided by the square root of the sample size (n):

$$\sigma\bar{x} = \frac{\sigma}{\sqrt{n}}$$

This describes the spread of the sample means around the population mean, decreasing as the sample size increases. Together, these equations summarize the behavior of sample means under the Central Limit Theorem.

### 2.2.4   correlation and causation

In statistics, correlation and causation are two of the most significant but perplexing concepts. While causation indicates that one event is caused by another, correlation shows the relationship between two variables. We shall talk about the distinction between correlation and causation in this article.

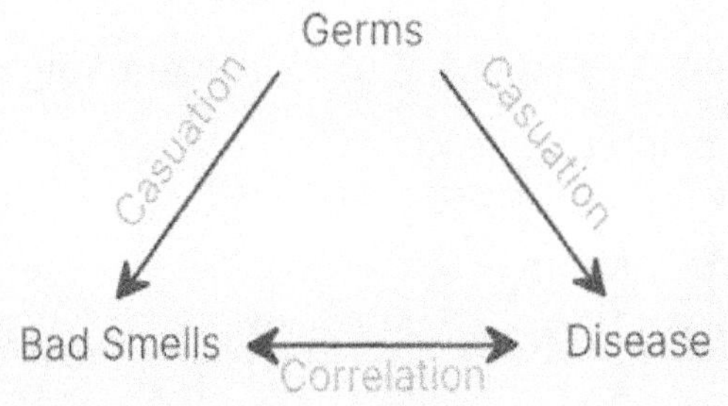

## Difference between Correlation and Causation

| Parameter | Correlation | Causation |
|---|---|---|
| Definition | Correlation means there is a relationship between the values of two variables. | Causation means one event causes another event to occur. |
| Relation | Correlation doesn't imply Causation. | Causation always implies Correlation. |
| Variable | Both Independent and Dependent variables are needed. | Both Independent and Dependent Variables are needed. |
| Example | Tiredness and Bad mood are correlated. | Tiredness and Bad mood are caused due to traffic jams. |

## 2.2.5  A/B testing

### What Do People Think A/B Testing Looks Like?

The simplified view suggests A/B testing is just choosing between two designs or options (A and B), then quickly selecting the better option (B) based on its performance. It's portrayed as a straightforward decision-making process with minimal complexity.

### What A/B Testing Actually Is?

This section reveals the true complexity of A/B testing. It depicts a cyclical, iterative process that involves multiple stages and steps. These include:

- ***Design Base Layout:*** Starting with a baseline version of what is being tested.
- ***Create Variations:*** Develop different versions (A and B) for comparison.
- ***Define Test Plan:*** Setting up the experiment, including determining metrics and sample size.
- ***Collect Data***: Running the test and gathering data on the performance of the variations.
- ***Run with Best Option:*** After analyzing the data, select the better-performing option.
- ***Set up another A/B Test:*** Repeating the process to optimize further, as A/B testing is often ongoing.

detailed breakdown of the process of the A/B test, the essential tasks such as

- *Defining goals and hypotheses*
- *Choosing relevant metrics*
- *Randomizing user assignment*
- *Testing for statistical significance*
- *Controlling for confounding variables*
- *Learning from results*

A/B Testing Factors to Consider

- ***Sample Size:*** For results to be dependable, it is important to have a sufficient sample size. Inconclusive or misleading results may arise from small sample sizes, while resource-intensive outcomes may result from too large samples.

- ***Duration of Testing:*** The validity of results is affected by the duration of A/B testing. While long periods might result in out-of-date findings, short ones can miss long-term trends.

- ***Variability* in User Behavior:** Variability may be introduced by a range of user behaviors. Useful analyses need an understanding of user segmentation and preferences.

- ***Selecting Useful Measures:*** It's critical to choose pertinent metrics that support the objectives of the experiment. The efficacy of the A/B testing procedure is guaranteed by concentrating on relevant indicators.

## Instruments and Methods for A/B Testing

✓ ***Google A/B Testing:***

Google Optimize has a user-friendly interface for setting tests and tracking performance, and it interacts easily with Google Analytics. This makes Google A/B Testing a feature-rich tool.

Use: Perfect for A/B testing on the web, offering insightful data on how users interact with various webpage elements.

✓ ***A/B Testing using Firebase:***

Features: Firebase A/B Testing, designed for mobile applications, lets developers test different app versions.

Application: This is especially helpful for boosting retention rates, evaluating engagement, and optimizing user experiences in mobile apps.

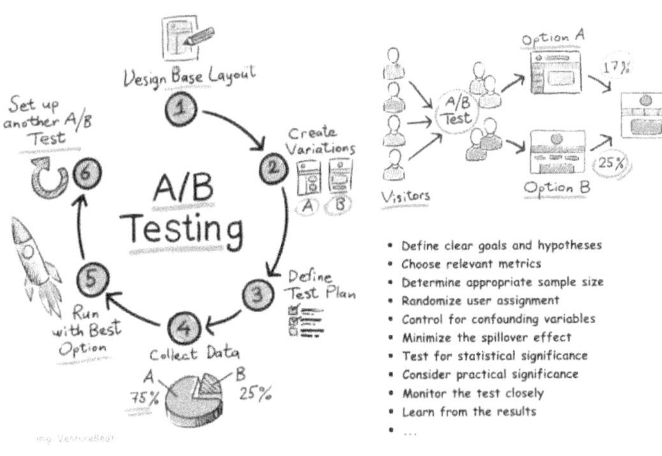

## 2.2.6  Confidence intervals

When estimating the population mean, like the average height of adults in a city, using a sample mean from a small sample (e.g., 10 people), the sample mean won't exactly equal the population mean due to sampling error. As the sample size increases, the sample mean gets closer to the population mean, but increasing the sample size indefinitely is impractical.

To account for the uncertainty in the estimate, we calculate a confidence interval, which provides a range of values likely to contain the population mean, based on sample statistics. The confidence interval is determined by adding and subtracting a margin of error from the sample mean.

The **confidence level** indicates the likelihood that the confidence interval contains the population mean. For example, with a 95% confidence level, if we repeated the sampling process multiple times, 95 out of 100 intervals would likely contain the population mean.

In **hypothesis testing**, the **significance level** represents the probability of rejecting a true null hypothesis. The common standard is 5%, meaning a confidence level of 95% is used. These two concepts are linked: rejecting a null hypothesis at a significance level of 0.05 corresponds to a 95% confidence level.

*Confidence level = 1 — Significance level (alpha)*

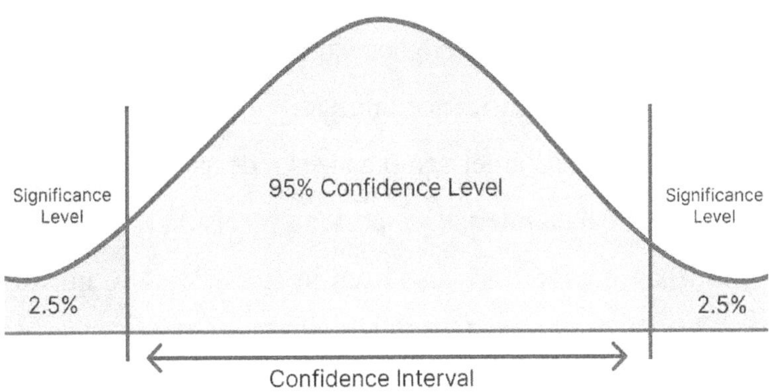


Confidence intervals are used to estimate the range within which a population parameter (e.g., mean or proportion) is likely to lie, given a sample from that population. The formula for continuous data uses the sample mean, critical z-value or t-value, sample standard deviation, and sample size to calculate the lower and upper limits of the interval, with the margin of error being the second term in the formula. For smaller samples ($n < 30$), t-values provide more accuracy.

For categorical data (e.g., estimating proportions), the confidence interval formula adjusts based on the sample proportion. In the example, a confidence interval for 60% of people being over 165 cm was calculated to be (0.58, 0.62), leading to a conclusion with 95% confidence that more than 50% of people are above 165 cm.

Factors influencing confidence intervals:

- ***Confidence level:*** A higher confidence level increases the range of the interval.

- ☐ *Sample variability:* Higher variability in the data results in a wider confidence interval.

- ☐ *Sample size:* Larger sample sizes reduce the width of the confidence interval, improving precision.

Confidence intervals are also used in A/B testing to quantify uncertainty around p-values in hypothesis testing.

## 2.2.7  T-tests & Z-test

*The T-test* is an inferential statistic used to determine if there is a significant difference between the means of two groups and how they are related. T-tests are used when the data sets follow a normal distribution and have unknown variances, like the data set recorded from flipping a coin 100 times.

- *Population standard deviation is unknown*
- *sample size is small, n < 30*
- *T-Test = $(\bar{x} - \mu) / (s / \sqrt{n})$*

$\sigma/\sqrt{n}$  *Standard Error*

*s  sample standard deviation*

*$\mu$ Population Mean*

*$\bar{x}$  Sample Mean*

*n No. of Sample*

- *Degrees of Freedom is n-1*
- *We Used a T-test when the population standard deviation is unknown, or the sample size is small.*

- *T-tests can be dependent or independent.*

*The Z-test* is also a hypothesis test in which the z-statistic follows a normal distribution. The z-test is best used for greater-than-30 samples because, under the central limit theorem, as the number of samples gets larger, the samples are approximately normally distributed.

*Population standard deviation is known.*

- *Large sample size (n > 30)*

- *Z-Test = $(\bar{x} - \mu) / (\sigma / \sqrt{n})$*

  *$\sigma/\sqrt{n}$ Standard Error*

  *$\sigma$  Population standard deviation*

  *$\mu$  Population Mean*

  *$\bar{x}$  Sample Mean*

  *n  No. of Sample*

- *Degrees of Freedom Not applicable*

- *We Used Z Test when the population standard deviation is known, and the sample size is large.*

❏ When are Z-tests and T-tests used?

A z-test is applied to test a null hypothesis when the population variance is known, or if the sample size is larger than 30 with an unknown population variance. In contrast, a t-test is used when the sample size is smaller than 30 and the population variance is unknown.

❑ What is the difference between a one-tailed and two-tailed Z-test?

A one-tailed z-test evaluates the possibility of rejecting the null hypothesis in only one direction, while a two-tailed z-test considers the potential for rejection in both directions (both left and right).

❑ What are the assumptions of the T-test and Z-test?

The z-statistic assumes a standard normal distribution, whereas the t-statistic assumes a t-distribution, with degrees of freedom equal to n-1, where n represents the sample size.

## 2.2.8  ANOVA

ANOVA, or Analysis of Variance, is a statistical test used to determine whether there are significant differences between the means of more than two groups. It does this by comparing the variation between group means to the variation within the groups. If the variation between the group means is significantly greater than the variation within the groups, it indicates a significant difference between the means. The test calculates an F-statistic by comparing between-group variability to within-group variability, and if the F-statistic exceeds a critical value, it confirms significant differences between the group means. ANOVA is commonly used to compare treatments, analyze the impact of various factors on a variable, or compare means across multiple groups. There are different types of ANOVA, including one-way ANOVA (for comparing the means of groups) and two-way ANOVA (which examines the effects of two independent variables on a dependent variable).

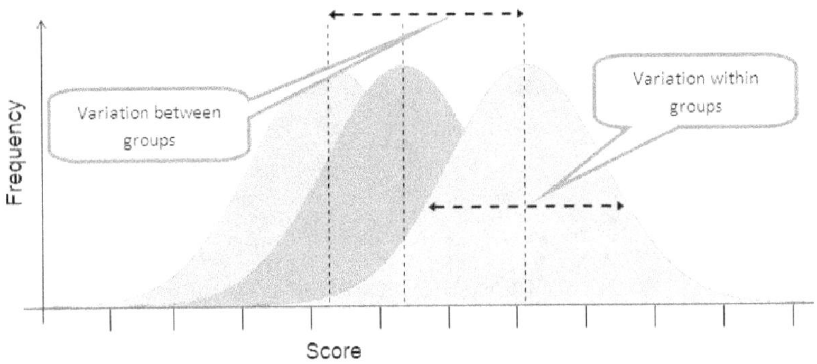


ANOVA is used for experimental data, particularly when statistical software is unavailable, as it can be manually calculated and is well-suited for small samples involving subjects or test groups. It functions similarly to multiple two-sample t-tests but with fewer type I errors. ANOVA compares group differences by evaluating group means and partitioning variance into different sources. A one-way ANOVA analyzes one independent and one dependent variable, while a two-way ANOVA involves two independent variables, each with at least three groups or categories. ANOVA helps determine whether the dependent variable changes based on the levels of the independent variable.

> **ANOVA Formula**
>
> $$F = \frac{MST}{MSE}$$
>
> **where:**
> $F$ = ANOVA coefficient
> $MST$ = Mean sum of squares due to treatment
> $MSE$ = Mean sum of squares due to error

## One-Way vs. Two-Way ANOVA

### *One-Way ANOVA*

- Uses one independent variable or factor.

- Assesses the impact of a single categorical variable on a continuous dependent variable, identifying significant differences among group means.

- Does not account for interactions.

### *Two-Way ANOVA*

- Uses two independent variables or factors.

- Used to not only understand the individual effects of two different factors but also how the combination of these two factors influences the outcome.

- Can test interactions between factors.

## 2.2.9  Common Statistical Tests

| Test | Purpose | When To Use | Applications in Finance/Investing |
|---|---|---|---|
| **ANCOVA** | Compare the arithmetical means of two or more groups while controlling for the effects of a continuous variable | • Normal distribution • Comparing multiple independent variables with a covariate | • Analyzing investment returns while controlling for market volatility • Evaluating the effectiveness of financial strategies while accounting for economic conditions |
| **ANOVA** | Compare the means of three or more groups | • Data is normally distributed | • Comparing financial performance across different sectors or investment strategies |
| **Chi-Square Test** | Test for association between two | • Data is categorical (e.g., | • Analyzing customer demographics and |

| Test | Purpose | When To Use | Applications in Finance/Investing |
|---|---|---|---|
| | categorical variables (can't be measured on a numerical scale) | investment choices, market segments) | portfolio allocations |
| Correlation | Measure the strength and direction of a linear relationship between two variables | • Data is continuous | • Assessing risk and return of assets, portfolio diversification |
| Durbin-Watson Test | Checks if errors in a prediction model are related over time | • Time series data | • Detecting serial correlation in stock prices, market trends |
| F-Test | Compare variances of two or more | • Data is normally distributed | • Testing the equality of variances in stock |

| Test | Purpose | When To Use | Applications in Finance/Investing |
| --- | --- | --- | --- |
| | groups | | returns and portfolio performance |
| Granger Causality Test | Test for a causal relationship between two-time series | • Time series data | • Determining if one economic indicator predicts another |
| Jarque-Bera Test | Test for normality of data | • Continuous data | • Assessing if financial data follows a normal distribution |
| Mann-Whitney U test | Compare medians of two independent samples | • Data is not normally distributed | • Comparing the financial performance of two groups with non-normal distributions |
| MANOVA | Compare means of two or more groups | • Data is normally distributed • | • Assessing the impact of different investment |

| Test | Purpose | When To Use | Applications in Finance/Investing |
| --- | --- | --- | --- |
| | on multiple dependent variables simultaneously | Analyzing multiple related outcome variables | portfolios on multiple financial metrics • Evaluating the overall financial health of companies based on various performance indicators |
| **One-Sample T-Test** | Compare a sample mean to a known population mean | • Data is normally distributed, or the sample size is large | • Comparing actual vs. expected returns |
| **Paired T-Test** | Compare means of two related samples (e.g., before and after | • Data is normally distributed, or the sample size | • Evaluating if a financial change has been effective |

# Data Scientist Roadmap

| Test | Purpose | When To Use | Applications in Finance/Investing |
| --- | --- | --- | --- |
| Regression | measurements) Predict the value of one variable based on the value of another variable | is large • Data is continuous | • Modeling stock prices • Predicting future returns |
| Sign Test | Test for differences in medians between two related samples | • Data is not normally distributed | • Non-parametric alternative to paired t-test in financial studies |
| T-Test | Compare the means of two groups | • Data is normally distributed, or the sample size is large | • Comparing the performance of two investment strategies |
| Wilcoxon Rank-Sum Test | Compare medians of two independent | • Data is not normally distributed | • Non-parametric alternative to independent t-test |

| Test | Purpose | When To Use | Applications in Finance/Investing |
|---|---|---|---|
| | samples | | in finance |
| Z-Test | Compare a sample mean to a known population mean | • Data is normally distributed, and population standard deviation is known | • Testing hypotheses about market averages |

## 2.2.10 Sample size

In market research, the word "sample size" refers to the total number of participants in a sample for a study. This sample was drawn from the general population and is thought to be typical of the population under investigation.

For example, we can test a new product on a sample size that is typical of the intended demographic to forecast how the people in that age group will respond to it.

In this instance, the number of people in that age range who will be polled is referred to as the sample size.

Determining the appropriate sample size involves using statistical formulas, starting with the selection of a significant benchmark based on the expected outcomes of the qualitative research. Researchers typically have two main approaches:

***Variable-Based Sampling:*** This approach focuses on tracking the measurement of specific variables and identifying indicators that reflect their changes. For example, to study consumer behavior, a researcher might monitor the frequency of visits to a retail store and use the weekly average visit frequency as an indicator. In specialized literature, this method is known as sampling the variables being investigated.

***Attribute-Based Sampling:*** This approach aims to evaluate specific attributes related to the marketing phenomenon under investigation. For example, a researcher might assess consumer preferences regarding the interior design of a retail space, focusing on various significant attributes. In specialized literature, this method is referred to as sampling based on the investigated characteristics.

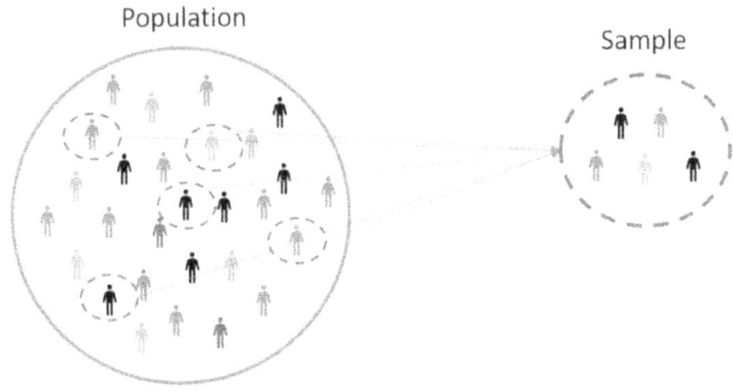

To practically apply the concepts of sample size determination, researchers use formulas that consider the expected effect size, the desired statistical power (typically 80% or higher), and the acceptable significance level (usually set at 5%). These calculations help ensure the sample size is adequate—neither too small to detect a significant effect nor too large, which would be inefficient.

## Sample Size Formula

$$N = \text{population size} \cdot e \cdot z$$

where:

- $e$ is the margin of error (expressed as a decimal),

- $z$ is the z-score.

Another widely used sample size formula is:

$$n = \frac{N \cdot X}{X + N - 1}$$

where:

- $X = \dfrac{Z^2_{\alpha/2} \cdot p \cdot (1-p)}{\text{MOE}^2}$,

- $Z_{\alpha/2}$ is the critical value of the normal distribution at $\alpha/2$ (for a 95% c[onfidence level] and the critical value is 1.96),

- MOE is the margin of error,

- $p$ is the sample proportion,

- $N$ is the population size.

# 2.2.11 Ways to Determine Data Normality

There are different techniques for evaluating data distributions, including:

- ❏ Plotting methods for visualization,
- ❏ Statistical tests to quantitatively assess distribution properties,
- ❏ Distance measures to quantify the similarity between distributions.

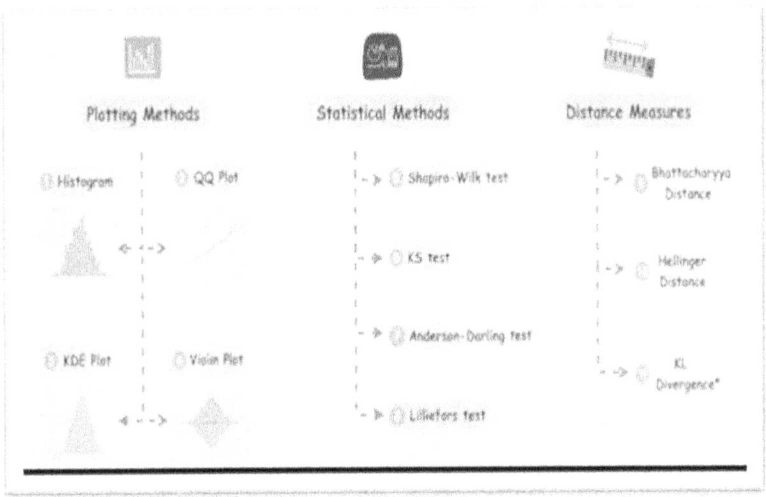


## Plotting Methods

⊙ ***Histogram:*** A graphical representation of the distribution of numerical data. It organizes data points into ranges (bins) and displays their frequency.

- ⊙ **QQ Plot:** Quantile-Quantile plot helps compare the distribution of a dataset with a theoretical distribution. Points on the plot should lie along a reference line if the data follows the same distribution.

- ⊙ **KDE Plot (Kernel Density Estimate):** A smoothed estimate of the probability density function of a random variable, used to visualize the distribution of data.

- ⊙ **Violin Plot:** Combines aspects of a box plot and a KDE plot, showing both the distribution and probability density of the data.

## Statistical Methods

- ⊙ **Shapiro-Wilk test:** A test that assesses the normality of a distribution. It tests whether a sample comes from a normally distributed population.

- ⊙ **KS Test (Kolmogorov-Smirnov Test):** Used to compare a sample distribution to a reference probability distribution (e.g., normal distribution) or to compare two sample distributions.

- ⊙ **Anderson-Darling Test:** A statistical test for normality that places more emphasis on the tails of the distribution.

- ⊙ ***Lilliefors Test:*** A variation of the KS test that adjusts for small sample sizes when the parameters of the distribution (like mean or standard deviation) are estimated.

## Distance Measures

- ⊙ ***Bhattacharyya Distance:*** Measures the overlap between two statistical samples or probability distributions. It's often used to assess the similarity between distributions.

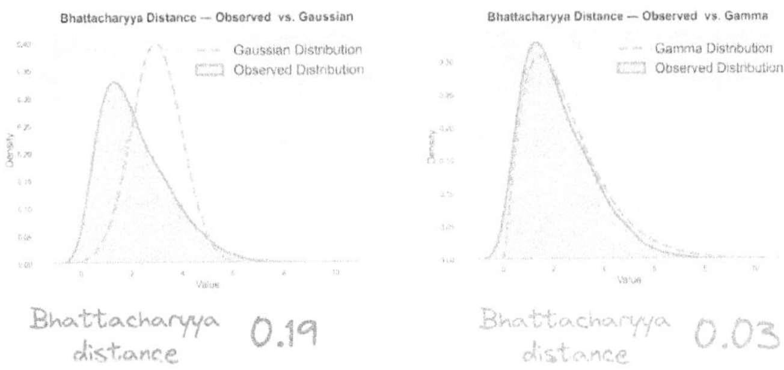


- ⊙ ***Hellinger Distance:*** Another measure of similarity between two probability distributions, often used in clustering and machine learning applications.

- ⊙ ***KL Divergence (Kullback-Leibler Divergence):*** A non-symmetric measure of the difference between two probability distributions. It tells you how one distribution diverges from another, often used in information theory and machine learning.

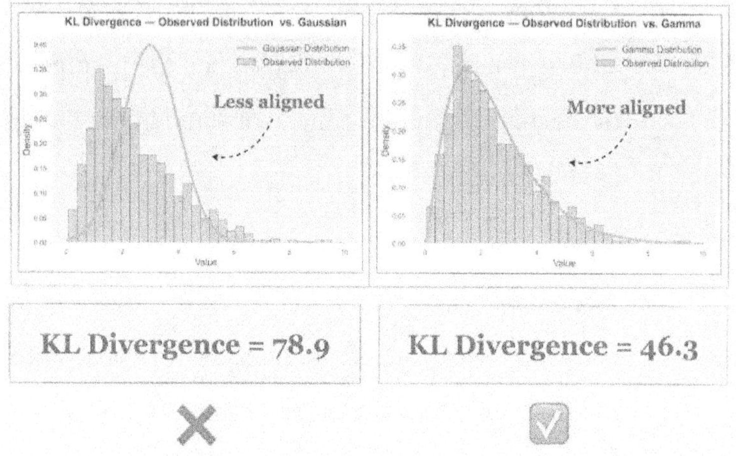


# 2.2.12 Probability vs. Likelihood

In data science and statistics, many people mistakenly use "probability" and "likelihood" interchangeably. This confusion is understandable because, in everyday language, the terms seem similar. For instance, according to the Cambridge Dictionary, *probability* is defined as "the level of possibility of something happening or being true," and *likelihood* is described as "the chance that something will happen." In fact, "likelihood" is often listed as a synonym for "probability." However, despite these overlapping definitions, it is essential to recognize that *probability* and *likelihood* are fundamentally different concepts in statistics and machine learning.

❑ Understanding Probability

Probability refers to the chance of a specific event occurring. It helps answer questions such as:

- What is the probability of rolling an even number on a die?
- What is the probability of drawing an ace of diamonds from a deck of cards?

In machine learning, probability is used similarly to assess the likelihood of certain classifications or outcomes. For example:

- What is the probability that a given transaction is fraudulent?
- What is the probability that an image contains a cat?

When working with probability, the model's parameters are known and are generally assumed to be accurate. For instance, when calculating the probability of a coin landing heads up, we typically assume the coin is fair (i.e., a 50% chance for heads).

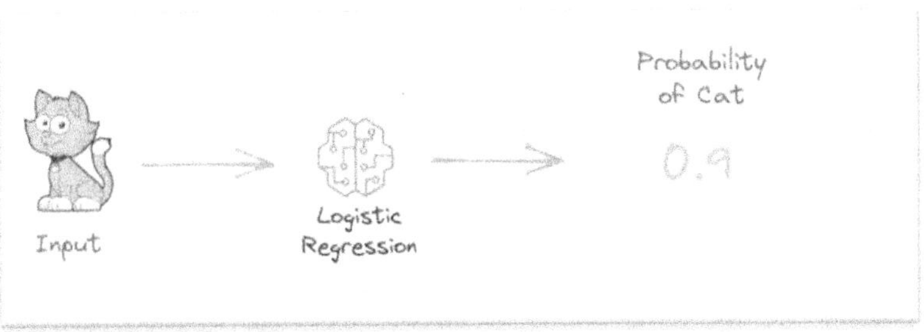


## ❑ Understanding Likelihood

Likelihood, on the other hand, focuses on explaining events

that have already occurred. While probability assumes the parameters are known and reliable, likelihood helps determine whether those parameters can be trusted, based on the observed data.

For example, imagine you have collected data and wish to model it using a straight line with parameters for slope (m) and intercept (c). Likelihood measures how well certain parameter values explain the observed data. In this case, you would ask questions like:

- Given the observed data, how well do the parameters m and c explain it?

This concept leads to the approach known as Maximum Likelihood Estimation (MLE). In MLE, observed data is used to identify the set of parameters ($\theta$) that maximize the likelihood of observing data.

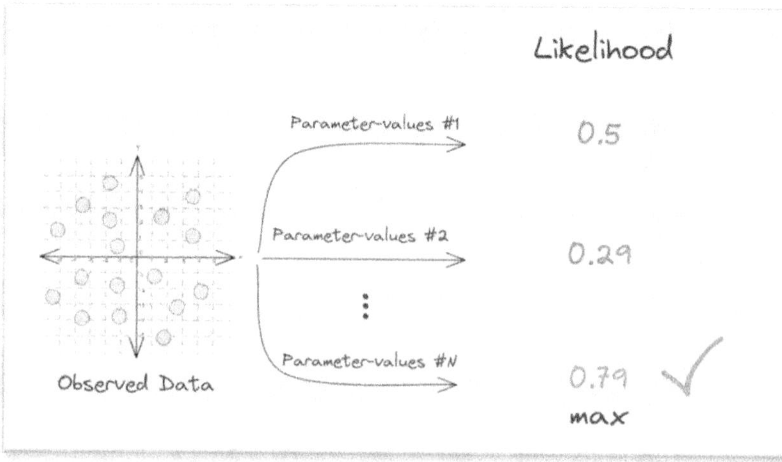

In practice, using the term *likelihood* is akin to saying:

- "I have a possible explanation for my data," where this explanation is represented by the parameters of your model.
- "How well does my explanation fit the data I've observed?"

For instance, imagine you observe the outcomes of 10-coin tosses, which result in "HHHHHHHTHH." You hypothesize that the coin is fair (P = 0.5). The likelihood would quantify how well this explanation (a fair coin) accounts for the observed data.

Summary of Key Differences

To summarize, it is critical to understand that probability and likelihood serve different purposes in data science:

- Probability is used to determine the chances of an event occurring, based on known and trusted parameters.
- Likelihood is used to evaluate whether the parameters of a model are trustworthy, based on observed data.

In other words, *probability* deals with predicting future events, while *likelihood* focuses on assessing how well an explanation (or model) fits existing data.

## 2.2.13 Probability Distributions in Data Science

### Uniform Distribution

All outcomes are equally likely within a given range. Often used in simulations and random sampling.

$$f(x) = \begin{cases} \dfrac{1}{b-a}, & x \in [a,b] \\ 0, & otherwise \end{cases}$$

### Normal Distribution

Also known as the Gaussian distribution, it's the famous bell curve where most observations cluster around the mean. It's widely used due to the Central Limit Theorem, making it crucial in fields like finance, social sciences, and natural sciences.

$$f(x) = \frac{1}{\sigma\sqrt{2\pi}} e^{-\frac{1}{2}\left(\frac{x-\mu}{\sigma}\right)^2}$$

### Binomial Distribution

Models the number of successes in a fixed number of independent trials, each with the same probability of success. Commonly used in quality control, survey analysis, and genetics.

$$P\left(X = x\right) = \frac{n!}{x!(n-x)!} p^{x} \left(1 - p\right)^{(n-x)}$$

❑ Poisson Distribution

Describes the number of events occurring within a fixed interval of time or space, given a constant mean rate. Used in queuing theory, telecommunications, and reliability engineering.

$$P(X) = \frac{\lambda^{x} e^{-\lambda}}{X!}$$

❑ Bernoulli Distribution

Represents a single trial with two possible outcomes: success or failure. The foundation for the binomial distribution is used in binary classification problems and A/B testing.

$$P(X = x) = \begin{cases} p & for\ x = 1 \\ 1 - p & for\ x = 0 \end{cases}$$

❑ Log-Normal Distribution

If a variable's logarithm is normally distributed, the variable itself is log-normally distributed. Commonly used in finance (e.g., modeling stock prices) and environmental data (e.g., distribution of pollutant concentrations).

$$X \sim N(\mu, \sigma^2) \qquad Y = e^X$$

$$Y \sim Lognormal(\mu, \sigma^2)$$

❏ Gamma Distribution

It models the time until an event occurs, such as the time until a system fails. It is widely used in survival analysis, reliability engineering, and insurance.

$$f(x; \alpha, \beta) = \begin{cases} \dfrac{1}{\beta^\alpha \Gamma(\alpha)} x^{\alpha-1} e^{-x/\beta} & x \geq 0 \\ 0 & \text{otherwise} \end{cases}$$

❏ Geometric Distribution

It models the number of trials until the first success in a sequence of independent Bernoulli trials. This is useful in reliability testing, risk analysis, and inventory management.

❏ Beta Distribution

Used to model the distribution of probabilities and is highly flexible due to its two shape parameters. Ideal for Bayesian inference, representing prior knowledge, and modeling events that have a natural boundary between 0 and 1.

$$\frac{x^{\alpha-1}(1-x)^{\beta-1}}{B(\alpha,\beta)}$$

where $B(\alpha,\beta) = \dfrac{\Gamma(\alpha)\Gamma(\beta)}{\Gamma(\alpha+\beta)}$ and $\Gamma$ is the Gamma function.

Each distribution has unique characteristics and applications, helping us to model real-world phenomena accurately. Whether it's predicting outcomes, estimating probabilities, or understanding variability, these distributions are indispensable tools in our data science toolkit.

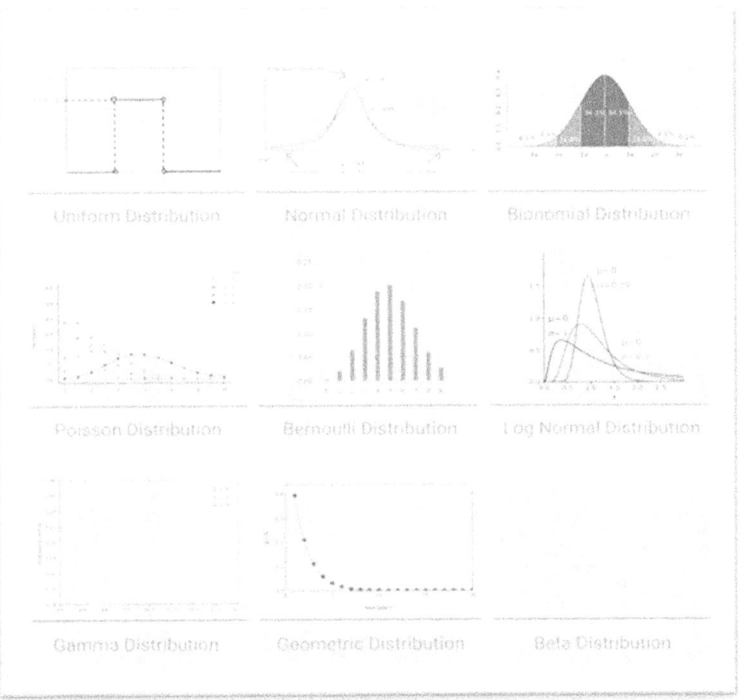

Thus, knowing some of the most important distributions and the type of data they can model is crucial.

Another visual below depicts the 11 most important distributions in data science:

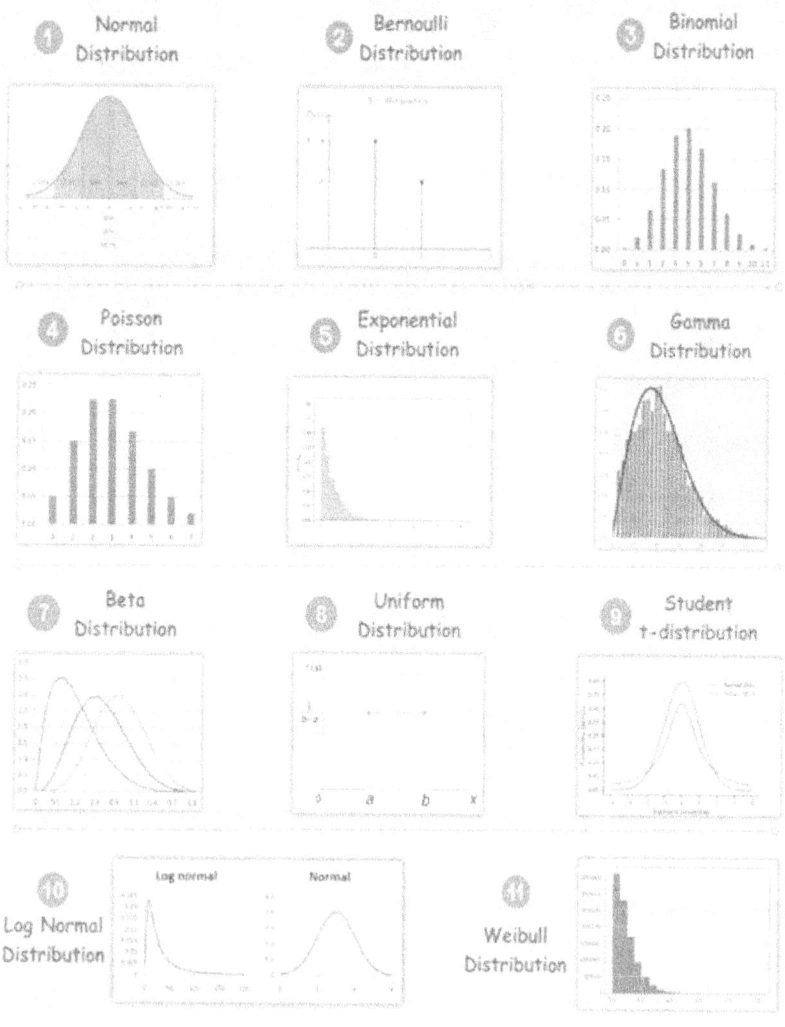

# 2.2.14 The Most Important Mathematical Definitions in DS

**1) Gradient Descent**

$$\theta_{j+1} = \theta_j - \alpha \nabla J(\theta_j)$$

**2) Normal distribution**

$$f(x|\mu,\sigma^2) = \frac{1}{\sigma\sqrt{2\pi}}\exp\left(-\frac{(x-\mu)^2}{2\sigma^2}\right)$$

**3) Z-score**

$$z = \frac{x-\mu}{\sigma}$$

**4) Sigmoid**

$$\sigma(x) = \frac{1}{1+e^{-x}}$$

**5) Correlation**

$$\text{Correlation} = \frac{\text{Cov}(X,Y)}{\text{Std}(X)\cdot\text{Std}(Y)}$$

**6) Cosine Similarity**

$$\text{similarity} = \frac{A\cdot B}{\|A\|\|B\|}$$

**7) Naive Bayes**

$$P(y|x_1,\ldots,x_n) = \frac{P(y)\prod_{i=1}^{n}P(x_i|y)}{P(x_1,\ldots,x_n)}$$

**8) MLE**

$$\text{argmax}_\theta \prod_{i=1}^{n} P(x_i|\theta)$$

**9) OLS**

$$\hat{\beta} = (X^T X)^{-1} X^T y$$

**10) F1 Score**

$$\frac{2\cdot P\cdot R}{P+R}$$

**11) ReLU**

$$\max(0, x)$$

**12) Softmax**

$$P(y = j|x) = \frac{e^{x^T w_j}}{\sum_{k=1}^{K} e^{x^T w_k}}$$

**13) R2 score**

$$R^2 = 1 - \frac{\sum_{i=1}^{n}(y_i - \hat{y}_i)^2}{\sum_{i=1}^{n}(y_i - \bar{y})^2}$$

**14) MSE**

$$\text{MSE} = \frac{1}{n}\sum_{i=1}^{n}(y_i - \hat{y}_i)^2$$

**15) MSE + L2 Reg**

$$\text{MSE}_{\text{regularized}} = \frac{1}{n}\sum_{i=1}^{n}(y_i - \hat{y}_i)^2 + \lambda\sum_{j=1}^{p}\beta_j^2$$

**16) Eigen vectors**

$$Av = \lambda v$$

**17) Entropy**

$$\text{Entropy} = -\sum_{i} p_i \log_2(p_i)$$

**18) KMeans**

$$\text{argmin}_S \sum_{i=1}^{k}\sum_{x\in S_i} \|x - \mu_i\|^2$$

**19) KL Divergence**

$$D_{KL}(P\|Q) = \sum_{x\in\mathcal{X}} P(x)\log\left(\frac{P(x)}{Q(x)}\right)$$

**20) Log-loss**

$$-\frac{1}{N}\sum_{i=1}^{N}\left(y_i\log(\hat{y}_i) + (1-y_i)\log(1-\hat{y}_i)\right)$$

**21) SVM**

$$\min_{w,b} \frac{1}{2}\|w\|^2 + C\sum_{i=1}^{n}\max(0, 1 - y_i(w\cdot x_i - b))$$

**22) Linear regression**

$$y = \beta_0 + \beta_1 x_1 + \beta_2 x_2 + \ldots + \beta_n x_n + \epsilon$$

**23) SVD**

$$A = U\Sigma V^T$$

# Chapter 3

# Machine Learning

## 3.1 Types of Machine Learning

- **Supervised learning:** In supervised learning, the algorithm is trained on labeled data, which means that the data includes both the input and the desired output. The algorithm learns to map the inputs to the outputs, which can then be used to make predictions on new, unseen data.

- **Unsupervised learning:** In unsupervised learning, the algorithm is trained on unlabeled data, which means that the data does not have any labels. The algorithm must learn to find patterns or structures in the data on its own. Unsupervised learning is often used for tasks such as clustering and dimensionality reduction.

- **Semi-supervised learning:** In semi-supervised learning, the algorithm is trained on a dataset that includes both labeled and unlabeled data. While the labeled data provides the input-output pairs, the unlabeled data helps the algorithm understand the structure of the input space. The algorithm leverages the combination of labeled and unlabeled data to learn a model that can make predictions on new, unseen data. This approach is particularly useful when labeling data is expensive or time-consuming.

❑ **Reinforcement learning:** In reinforcement learning, the algorithm learns by interacting with its environment. The algorithm receives rewards or penalties for its actions, and it must learn to take actions that maximize its rewards. Reinforcement learning is often used for tasks such as game playing and robot control.

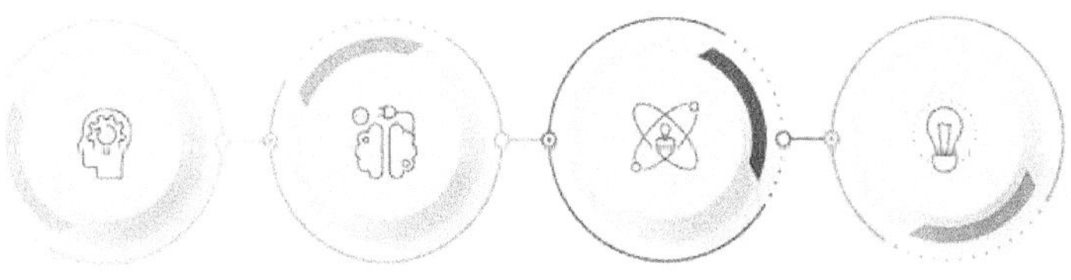

## 3.2  How to Choose the Right Machine Learning Model

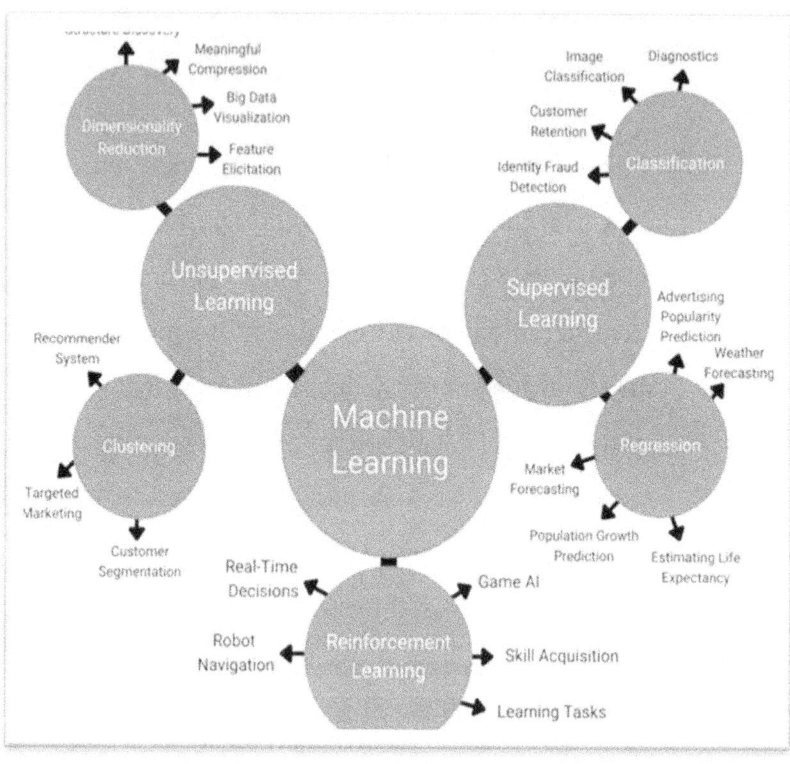


This figure provides an overview of machine learning, categorizing it into its main types, supervised, unsupervised, and reinforcement learning.

Supervised learning involves training algorithms on labeled data to make predictions (e.g., classification, regression). Unsupervised learning discovers patterns in unlabeled data (e.g., clustering, dimensionality reduction). Reinforcement learning trains agents to make decisions by interacting with an environment and receiving rewards or penalties.

The figure also highlights common applications within each category, such as image classification, customer segmentation, and market forecasting. It further explores concepts like feature elicitation, data visualization, and real-time decision-making.

In essence, this diagram illustrates the breadth of machine learning techniques and their diverse applications across various fields.

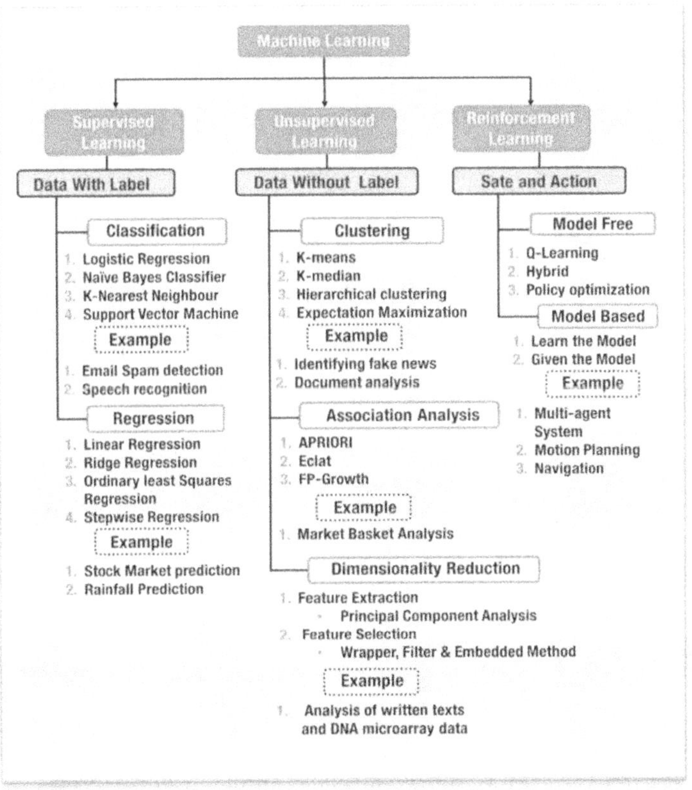

To provide readers with a comprehensive understanding of these categories and their applications in practical settings, the previous figure also includes additional sorts of machine learning algorithms and approaches, along with a few examples about each category.

## 3.3  Feature selection

Feature selection is the process of selecting a subset of relevant features from a larger set of variables or predictors in a dataset. It aims to improve model performance, reduce overfitting, enhance interpretability, and optimize computational efficiency. Here's an overview of the process and its importance.

*Importance of Feature Selection* Improved Model Performance: By selecting the most relevant features, the model can focus on the most informative variables, leading to better predictive accuracy and generalization.

*Overfitting Prevention* Including irrelevant or redundant features can lead to overfitting, where the model learns noise or specific patterns in the training data that do not generalize well to new data. Feature selection mitigates this risk.

*Interpretability and Insights* A smaller set of selected features makes interpreting and understanding the model's results easier, facilitating insights and actionable conclusions.

**Computational Efficiency** Working with a reduced set of features can significantly improve computational efficiency, especially when dealing with large datasets.

❑ Feature Selection Techniques:

| FS method | Strengths | Gaps |
|---|---|---|
| Filter method | Efficient and computationally faster. Independent of the learning algorithm. Computationally faster than the Wrapper and Embedded methods. Suitable for low-dimensional data. | It does not consider the correlation between classifiers. It does not consider the correlation between the features. Fails to recognize the patterns properly during the learning phase |
| Wrapper method | It considers the correlation between the features and class labels. Also Considers the dependencies between the features. More accurate than the Filter method. | Computationally more complex Iteratively evaluate the selected feature subset. Some features may not be considered for evaluation when dropped at the initial stage. Searching overhead. Causes overfitting |
| Embedded method | Computationally more efficient than the Wrapper method. More accurate than Filter and Wrapper method | Computationally costlier than the filter method. Not suitable for high dimensional data. Poor generality |

Stages in the Feature Selection process, are shown below:

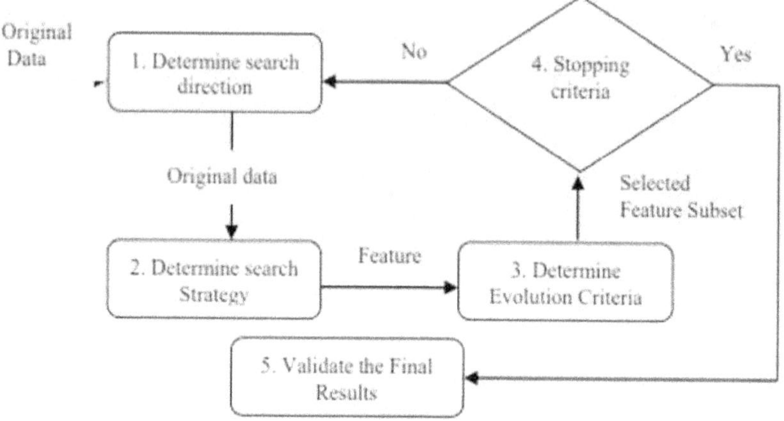


**The probe Method:** A reliable Feature Selection Technique

□ *Step 1:* **Add Random Feature**

Introduce a random feature (noise) to the original dataset. This helps differentiate between truly informative features and those that are just noise.

□ *Step 2*: **Train Model**

Train a machine learning model on the dataset with the added random feature.

□ *Step 3*: **Measure Feature Importance**

Evaluate the importance of each feature, including the random one, using techniques like permutation importance or SHAP values.

□ *Step 4*: **Filter Features**

Discard features with low importance, including the random

feature, as they are likely not to contribute significantly to the model's predictions.

## ❏ Step 5: Repeat Until Convergence

Purpose: Iterate through steps 1-4 multiple times, refining the feature set with each iteration. The process stops when the selected features stabilize (converge).

The Probe Method is a simple yet effective way to identify and remove irrelevant features from a dataset, improving model performance and interpretability.

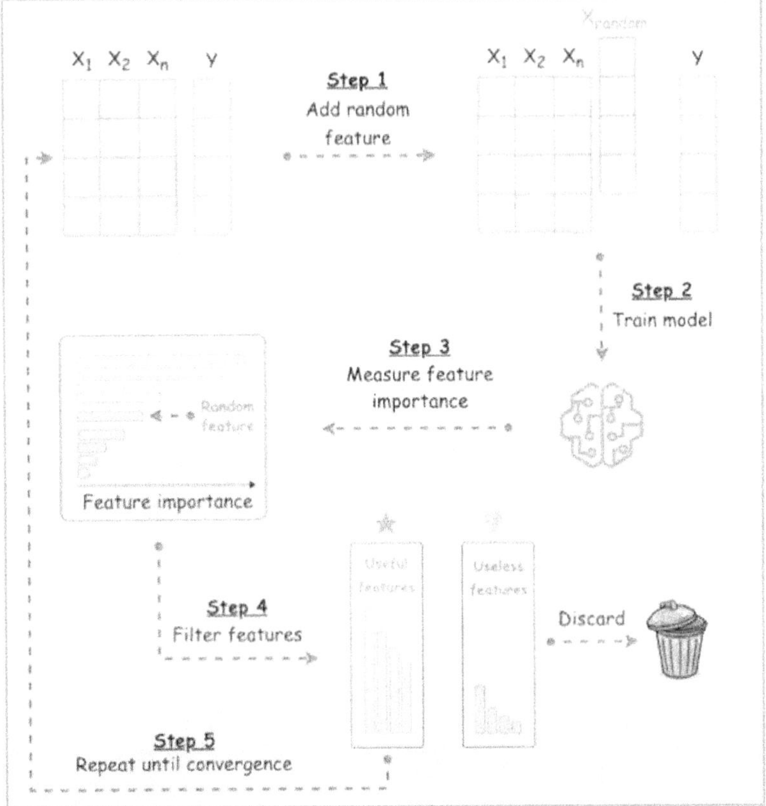

## 3.4  Model Selection

It involves employing a range of tools and libraries to fit various machine learning models on a given predictive modeling dataset. The true challenge lies in deciding which of the many models you can use to address your problem.

**"The process of selecting the machine learning model most appropriate for a given issue is known as model selection."**

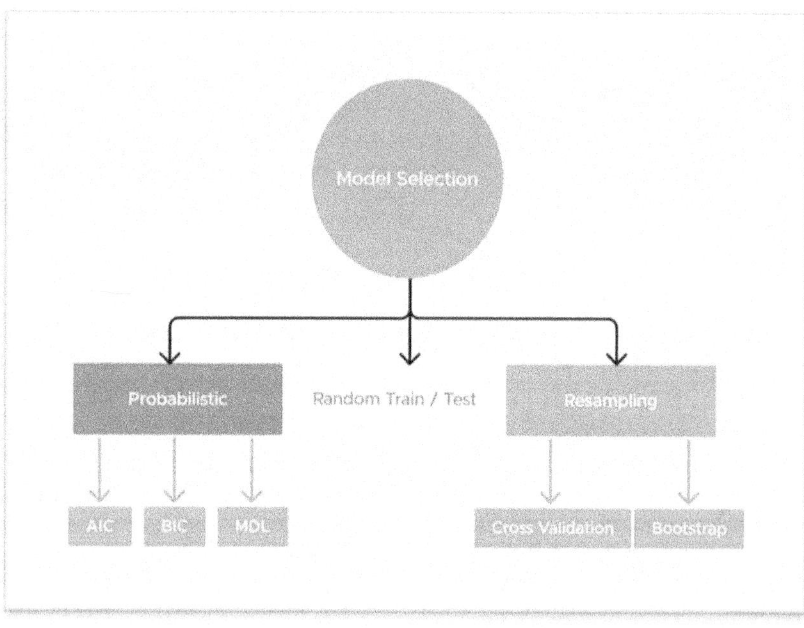


The dataset, task, model type, and other factors all have an impact on the model selection.

In general, there are two things to consider:

- The rationale behind selecting a model.

- The performance of the model

Now let's examine the rationale behind model selection. Models can be selected according to their data and task:

## 3.4.1 probabilistic

Information Criterion (IC) is a probabilistic measure used to evaluate the effectiveness of statistical models by scoring them based on a log-likelihood framework using Maximum Likelihood Estimation (MLE). Unlike resampling, which focuses solely on model performance, probabilistic modeling considers both performance and model complexity.

IC provides a score, with the lowest score indicating the most effective model. This score is calculated using all training data, without the need for a test set. Simpler models with fewer parameters are preferred, as they are easier to learn and maintain, though they may struggle with detecting performance fluctuations.

Three methods to calculate model fit and complexity are:

> **Akaike Information Criterion (AIC):** AIC is a numerical score used to compare models on the same dataset. Lower AIC scores indicate better model fit, factoring in accuracy and a penalty for complexity. However, AIC may favor more complex models that retain training data, potentially leading to poor generalization.

- **Minimum Description Length (MDL):** MDL is based on the principle that the best explanation allows for the most data compression. It underpins statistical modeling, pattern recognition, and machine learning, focusing on the number of bits required to describe both the model and its predictions.

- **Bayesian Information Criterion (BIC):** BIC, derived from Bayesian probability, is used for models trained with maximum likelihood estimation. It also balances model fit with complexity, like AIC but with a different penalty term.

IC methods like AIC, MDL, and BIC are essential tools in model selection, helping to balance model accuracy with complexity.

## 3.4.2 Resampling

Resampling methods are techniques used to evaluate the performance and generalizability of machine learning models by testing them on different samples of data. The two main types of resampling methods are:

- **Cross-Validation:** This method splits the data into multiple groups, where one group is used as test data while the others are used for training. The model's performance is evaluated across different iterations, and the mean accuracy is calculated. This process helps in comparing different models, such as SVM and logistic regression, to determine which one performs better.

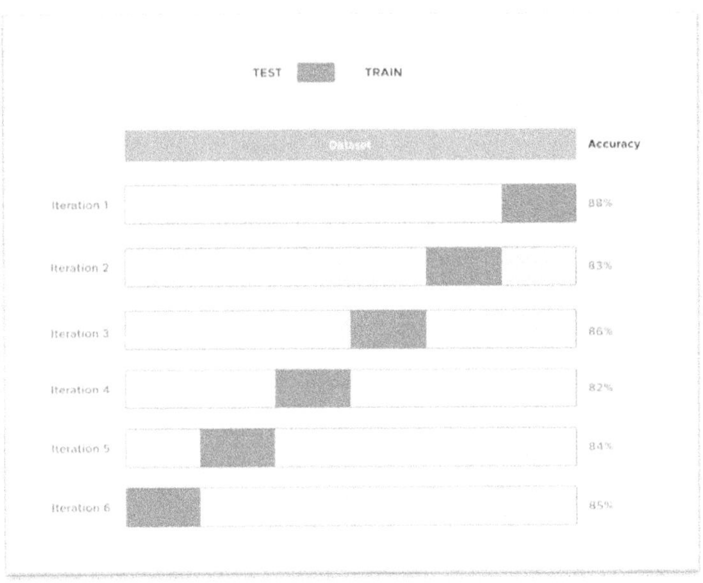



**Bootstrap**: This technique involves randomly sampling data with replacement to create new datasets. It's particularly useful for smaller datasets and helps estimate statistics on a population. The process involves selecting observations, noting them, replacing them, and repeating the steps multiple times. The result is a bootstrap sample with the same number of observations as the original dataset.

## 3.5  Train and Test Split

You must divide your data into three parts to train a machine learning model: the train set, the test set, and the validation set. The validation set is used to adjust the model's hyperparameters, the test set is used to assess the model, and the train set is used to train the model.

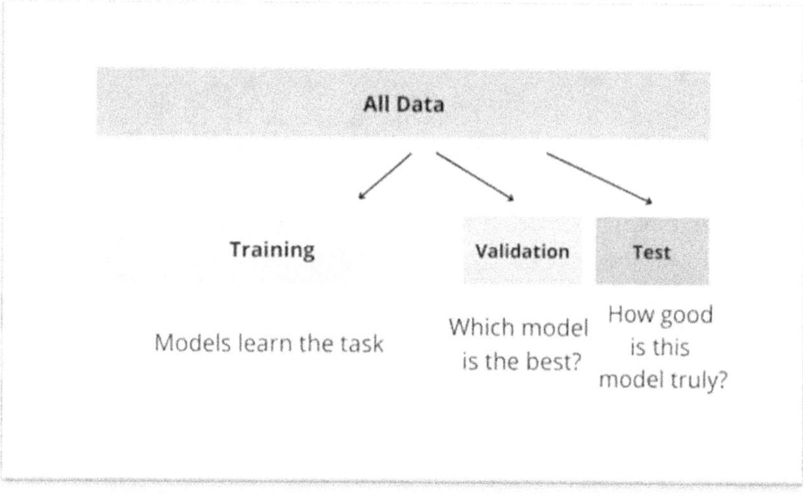


The objective of dividing our data into three segments is:

We must divide our data into three sets to prevent our model from overfitting the training set. When a model becomes overfit, it can no longer generalize to new data since it has learned the training set too thoroughly. We can assess the model's performance on fresh data using the test set, and we can adjust the model's hyperparameters to prevent the model from overfitting to the training set.

- **Train Dataset**: The training dataset is like a learning tool for a robot to identify fruits. It includes labeled pictures of fruits that help the robot recognize patterns like shape, color, and texture, improving its ability to distinguish between different fruits.

- **Validation Dataset**: The validation dataset is used to fine-tune the robot's performance. After training, the robot is given more fruit pictures to validate its accuracy. If it makes mistakes, adjustments are made to improve its fruit recognition abilities.

- **Test Dataset**: The test dataset checks the robot's fruit identification skills with new, unseen pictures. It's used to evaluate how well the robot can apply its training to correctly identify new fruits.

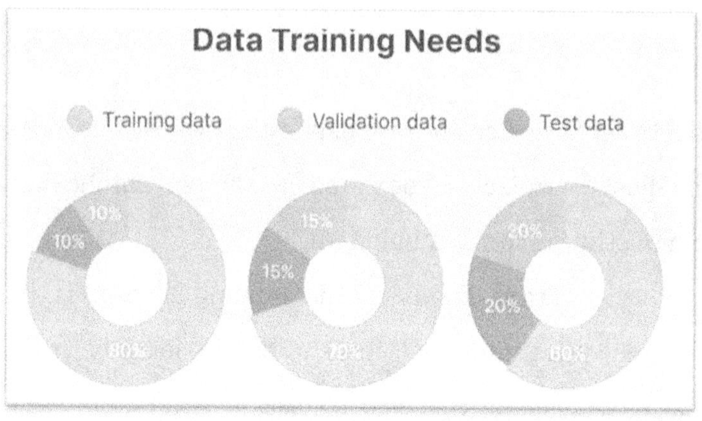


## 3.6  Model Evaluation

# 3.6.1  K-fold Validation Techniques

❑ Data Splitting

> <u>Shuffle the Dataset Randomly:</u>

✓ Before splitting, shuffle the dataset to ensure that the division into folds is unbiased.

> <u>Define the Dataset:</u>

✓ Let the dataset be D with N samples.

> <u>Choose the Number of Folds:</u>

✓ Select a value for K, which represents the number of folds.

> <u>Split the Dataset:</u>

✓ Divide D into K subsets (D1, D2,…,DK), where each subset contains approximately N/K samples.

❑ Cross-Validation Process

➢ <u>For each fold i (where i=1, 2,,K).</u>

✓ Validation Set: Assign the subset Di as the validation set.

✓ Training Set: Use the remaining data D/Di (all data in D except Di) as the training set.

➢ <u>Model Training and Evaluation:</u>

✓ Train the model on D/Di.

✓ Test the trained model on Di.

✓ Record Performance: Save the performance score as Si.

❑ Calculating Performance Metrics

➢ <u>Aggregate the Scores:</u>

Collect the performance scores S1, S2,, and SK from all folds.

➢ <u>Calculate the Mean Score:</u>

✓ Mean Score=

$$\frac{\sum_{i=1}^{K} S_i}{K} .$$

➢ <u>Calculate the Standard Deviation (Optional):</u>

✓ Standard Deviation SD=

$$\sqrt{\frac{\sum_{i=1}^{K}(S_i-\text{Mean})^2}{K}}.$$

❏ Interpretation

➢ <u>Mean Score:</u>

✓ Represents the average performance of the model across all folds, giving an overall measure of its effectiveness.

➢ <u>Standard Deviation:</u>

✓ Provides insight into the consistency of the model's performance across different subsets of data. A lower standard deviation indicates more consistent performance.

➢ <u>Advantages of K-Fold Cross-Validation:</u>

✓ Every data point is used both for training and validation, ensuring that the model is thoroughly evaluated.

✓ Particularly beneficial when working with smaller datasets where a separate hold-out test set might not be feasible.

✓ By averaging performance across different subsets, K-fold cross-validation offers a balanced perspective on how the model might perform on unseen data.

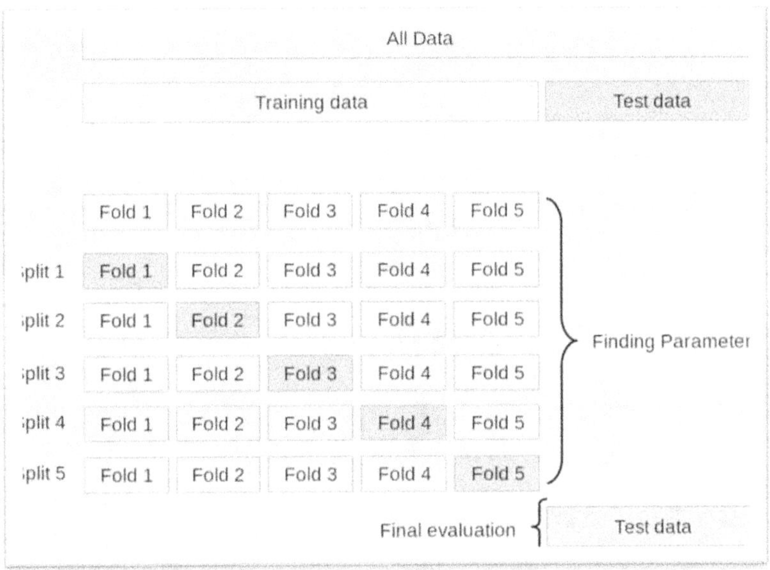


## 3.6.2 Bias-Variance trad-off

❑ bias

➢ The bias of the estimated function indicates how well the underlying model can predict the values.

➢ The error between average model prediction and ground truth

❑ Variance

➢ The variance of the estimated function indicates how much the function can adapt to changes in the dataset.

> Average variability in the model prediction for the provided dataset.

### High Bias

- Overly Simplified Model
- Under-fitting
- High error on both test and train data

### High Variance

- Overly complex Model.
- Over-fitting.
- Low error on train data and high on test.
- Starts modeling the noise in the input.

### Bias variance Trade-off

- Increasing bias (not always) reduces variance and vice-versa
- Error = bias2 + variance +irreducible error
- The best model is where the error is reduced.
- Compromise between bias and variance.

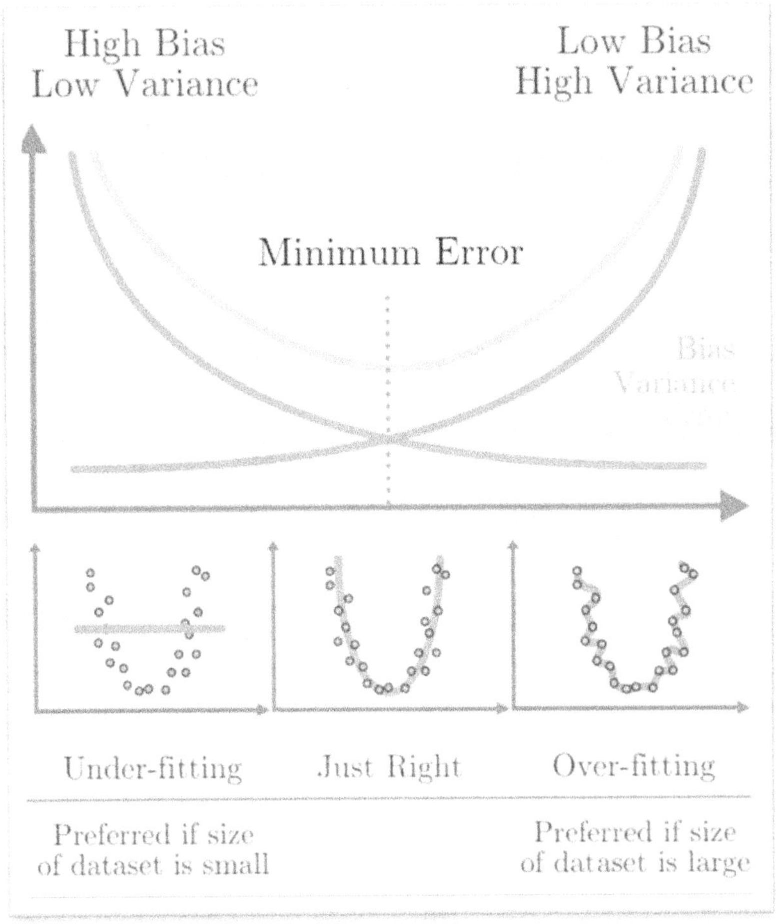


## 3.6.3 Confusion Matrix

With N representing the number of target classes, a confusion matrix is a N x N matrix used to assess a classification model's performance. By using a matrix, the machine learning model's projected values are compared with the real target values.

| | | Predicted | |
|---|---|---|---|
| | | **Negative (N)**<br>- | **Positive (P)**<br>+ |
| **Actual** | Negative<br>- | True Negative (TN) | **False Positive (FP)**<br>**Type I Error** |
| | Positive<br>+ | **False Negative (FN)**<br>**Type II Error** | True Positive (TP) |

✓ The target variable has two value **Positive** or **Negative**

✓ The **columns** represent the **actual values** of the target variable.

✓ The **rows** represent the **predicted values** of the target variable.

✓ **True Positives (TP)**: when the actual value is Positive and the predicted is also Positive.

✓ **True negatives (TN)**: when the actual value is Negative, and the prediction is also Negative.

✓ **False positives (FP)**: When the actual is negative, but the prediction is Positive. Also known as the **Type 1 error.**

✓ **False negatives (FN)**: When the actual is Positive, but the prediction is Negative. Also known as the **Type 2 error.**

## 3.6.4 The ROC Curve

The ROC curve is a graph that illustrates, at different thresholds, how successfully a classification model differentiates between two classes (e.g., "spam" and "not spam"). It allows you to see the model's performance at EVERY threshold that might be used, not just one.

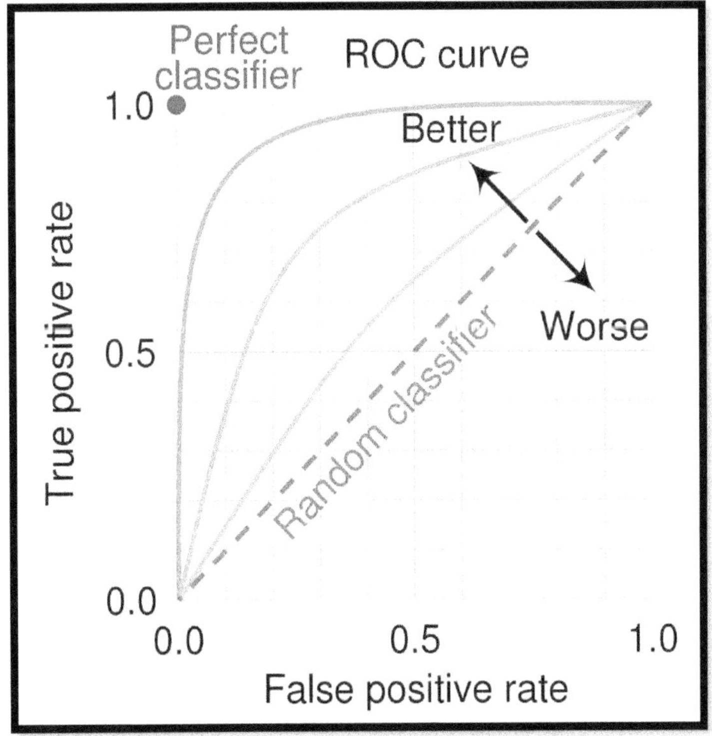

Top-Left Corner is Best: If the curve is closer to the top-left corner, that's great! It means we're correctly identifying spam without mislabeling many genuine emails. (Maximum True Positives, minimum false positives).

The ROC curve graphically evaluates binary classification models.

❑ *True Positive Rate (TPR):*

- A proportion of actual positives are correctly identified.
- Example: In a medical test, TPR indicates how many sick people are correctly diagnosed.

❑ *False Positive Rate (FPR):*

- A proportion of actual negatives are incorrectly identified as positives.
- Example: In a medical test, FPR shows how many healthy people are wrongly diagnosed.

❑ *Threshold Levels:*

- ROC curve plotted by changing the threshold, the cut-off points for class decisions.
- Lowering the threshold increases both true and false positives.
- Raising the threshold reduces false positives but may miss true positives.

- ***Shape of the ROC Curve:***

  - A curve closer to the top left corner indicates good performance (high TPR, low FPR).
  - A curve near the diagonal line indicates less effective performance.

- ***Area Under the Curve (AUC):***

  - A single number summarizing model performance.
  - A larger AUC indicates a better model. An AUC of 1 is perfect, while 0.5 suggests no discriminative ability.

- How to interpret the RUC curve

  - *Top-Left Corner is Best:* If the curve is closer to the top-left corner, that's great! It means we're correctly identifying spam without mislabeling many genuine emails. (Maximum True Positives, minimum false positives)
  - *Above the Diagonal Line:* If the curve is above the diagonal line (from bottom-left to top-right), our model is better than just random guessing because the diagonal line means where TPR = FPR.
  - *Area Under Curve (AUC):* The bigger the area under the curve (closer to 1), the better our model is.

### 3.6.5 Accuracy Metrics

A group of measurements called accuracy metrics are employed to assess how well categorization algorithms work. Aspects like the model's recall, precision, and accuracy are evaluated using these measures. It is frequently used to assess various models' side by side or fine-tune one model for best results. The three primary categories into which these measurements can be divided are accuracy, sensitivity, and specificity. Accuracy is the most significant parameter since it gauges the model's overall performance. Sensitivity and specificity gauge a model's ability to discriminate between several classes. Lastly, additional metrics that assess the accuracy and recognition of the model include the AUC score, F1 score, and Kappa score.

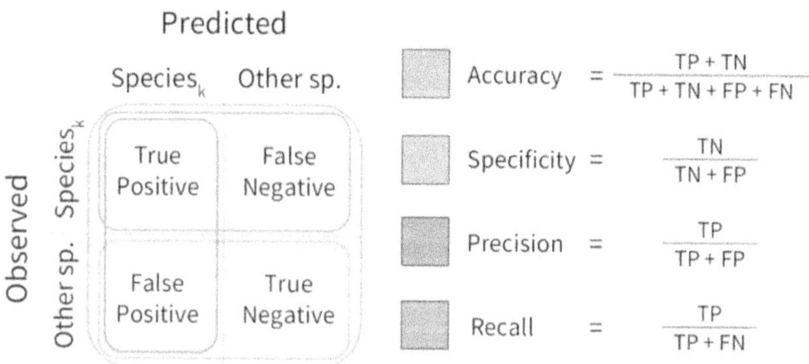



$$Accuracy = \frac{TP + TN}{TP + TN + FP + FN}$$

$$Specificity = \frac{TN}{TN + FP}$$

$$Precision = \frac{TP}{TP + FP}$$

$$Recall = \frac{TP}{TP + FN}$$

⊙ *Accuracy*: The accuracy metric measures the percentage of correctly classified instances. It is a good indicator of how well the model is performing, as it is easy to interpret and compare with other models.

- ⊚ ***Precision:*** Precision measures the number of true positives divided by the number of true positives plus false positives. It is the ability of the model to correctly classify positive examples.

- ⊚ ***Recall:*** Recall measures the number of true positives divided by the number of true positives plus false negatives. It is the ability of the model to identify all relevant instances.

- ⊚ ***F1 Score:*** The F1 score is the harmonic mean of precision and recall, and it is a convenient metric for comparing different models.

- ⊚ ***ROC Curve:*** The Receiver Operating Characteristic (ROC) curve plots the true positive rate (TPR) against the false positive rate (FPR). It is a good way to assess the performance of a model, especially for imbalanced datasets.

- ⊚ ***AUC:*** The Area Under the Curve (AUC) is the area under the ROC curve. It is a measure of the model's performance, and it can be used to compare different models.

## 3.6.6 Regularization

❑ The Concept

- Regularization is an approach to address over-fitting in ML.

- The overfitted model fails to generalize estimations on test data.

- When the underlying model to be learned is low bias/high variance, or when we have a small amount of data, the estimated model is prone to overfitting.

- Regularization reduces the variance of the model.

❑ Types of Regularization

- ***Modify the loss function:***
  - **L2 Regularization:** Prevents the weights from getting too large (defined by L2 norm). The larger the weights, the more complex the model is the more chances of overfitting.
  - **L1 Regularization:** Prevents the weights from getting too large (defined by L1 norm). The larger the weights, the more complex the model is, and the more chances of overfitting. L1 regularization introduces sparsity in the weights. It forces more weights to be zero than reducing the average magnitude of all weights.

- **Entropy**: Used for the models that output probability. Forces the probability distribution towards uniform distribution.

■ *Modify data sampling:*

- **Data augmentation:** Create more data from available data by randomly cropping, dilating, rotating, adding a small amount of noise, etc.
- **K-fold Cross-validation:** Divide the data into k groups. Train on (k-1) groups and test on 1 group. Try all k possible combinations.

■ *Change training approach:*

- **Injecting noise:** Add random noise to the weights when they are being learned. It pushes the model to be relatively insensitive to small variations in the weights, hence regularization.
- **Dropout**: Generally used for neural networks. Connections between consecutive layers are randomly dropped based on a dropout-ratio and the remaining network is trained in the current iteration. In the next iteration, another set of random connections is dropped.

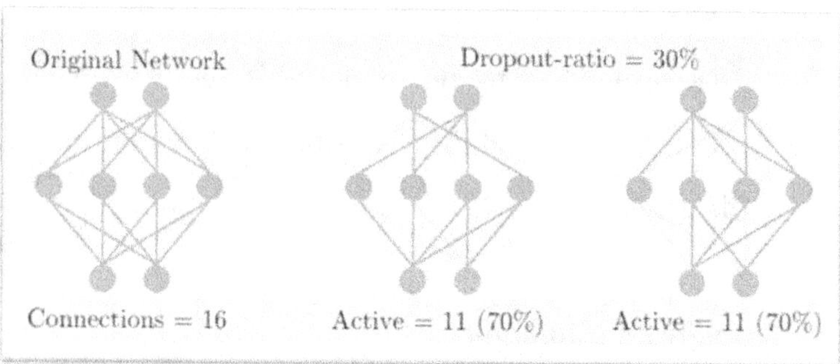


### 3.6.7 Normalization

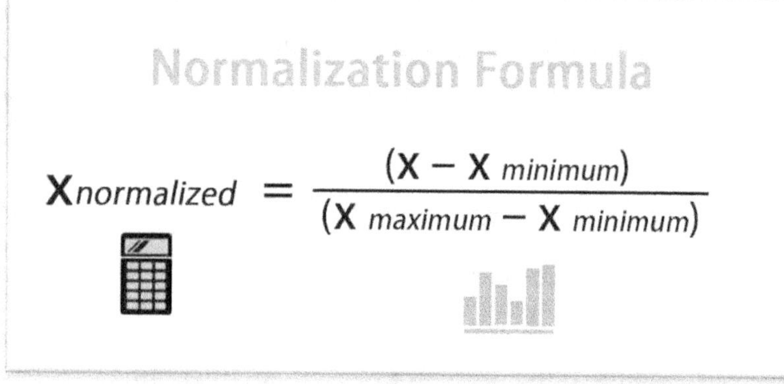


$$X_{normalized} = \frac{(X - X_{minimum})}{(X_{maximum} - X_{minimum})}$$

The primary goal of the normalization technique, which is frequently used in machine learning data preparation, is to convert the dataset's numeric column values to a standard scale without distorting the differences between the value ranges. It is not necessary to normalize every dataset. Only in cases where variables have discrete intervals is it required.

Take the dataset with the two attributes of age (x1) and income (x2), for example. The income ranges from 0 to 20,000 or more, while the age goes from 0 to 100 years. Age is nearly a thousand times less variable in value than income, which also varies far more greatly.

These two features are therefore at drastically different intervals. The specified income will have a major impact on the results of our further investigations, such as multivariate linear regression, because of its higher value. Additionally, this makes algorithm training challenging. MinMaxScaler is the name for normalization. The interval is set between 0 and 1 (or -1 and 1 if there are negative values) since it narrows the range of the data. It functions well in situations where uniformity might not be as effective. MinMaxScaler performs best when the distribution is not Gaussian, or the standard deviation is too small.

The main algorithms that require normalization are those that use distance measurements, such as clustering and cosine similarity-based recommendation systems. Because the variable is on a bigger scale, normalization prevents it from affecting the outcome.

## <u>Some algorithms that Need to Be Normalized</u>

- KNN with Euclidean distance measurement.
- Neural networks, SVM, and logistic regression.
- K-Means.

- Principal component analysis (PCA), kernel principal component analysis, and linear discriminant analysis.

## 3.7 Overfitting and underfitting

Overfitting and underfitting are two common problems that occur in machine learning and statistical models, affecting their performance on new, unseen data. They represent opposite ends of the spectrum regarding model complexity and how well the model generalizes to new data.

## 3.7.1 Overfitting

Overfitting occurs when a model learns the detail and noise in the training data to the extent that it negatively impacts the model's performance on new data. This means the model is too complex, capturing noise and patterns that do not generalize well outside of the training set.

- **Characteristics:** - High accuracy on training data but poor accuracy on test/unseen data. - The model has too many parameters or too much flexibility. - It captures random fluctuations in the training data as if they were important patterns.

- **Prevention and Solutions:** - Simplify the model by selecting a less complex model or reducing the number of parameters. - Use techniques like regularization (L1, L2) to penalize overly complex models. - Employ cross-validation to assess model performance on unseen data. - Collect more training data to help the model generalize better. - Use techniques like pruning in decision trees to remove parts of the model that do not contribute much to its predictive power.

## 3.7.2 Underfitting

Underfitting occurs when a model is too simple to learn the underlying structure of the data. This means the model does not Data Science fit the training data well and, as a result, cannot perform well on new data either.

- ⊙ **Characteristics:** - Poor performance on both training and test data. - The model has too few parameters or too little flexibility to capture the underlying trends of the data. - It fails to capture important patterns or relationships in the data.

- ⊙ **Prevention and Solutions**: - Increase model complexity by selecting a more complex model or adding more parameters. - Feature engineering to introduce more relevant features that can help the model learn better. - Reduce the amount of regularization if it's too high and constrain the model excessively.

**Key Difference:** The key difference between overfitting and underfitting lies in the model's complexity and its performance on training versus new data. Overfitting involves a complex model that performs well on training data but poorly on new data, while underfitting involves a too-simple model that performs poorly on both training and new data. Achieving a balance between the two, where the model is complex enough to learn the underlying patterns but not so complex that it learns the noise, is key to building models that generalize well to unseen data.

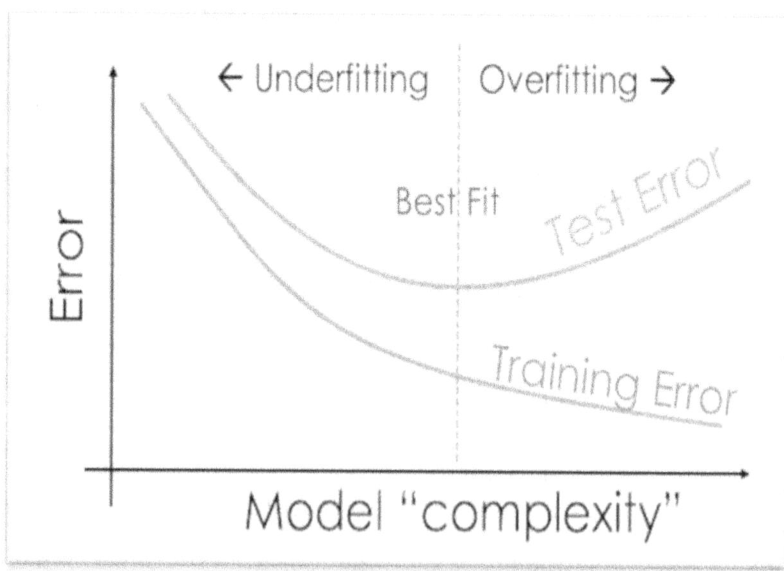

## 3.8 Autoencoder and Variational Autoencoder

### 3.8.1 Auto Encoder (AE)

- Autoencoder is used to learn efficient embeddings of unlabeled data for a given network configuration. It consists of two parts, an encoder, and a decoder.

- The encoder compresses the data from a higher-dimensional space to a lower-dimensional space (also called the latent space), while the decoder converts the latent space back to a higher-dimensional space.

- The entire encoder-decoder architecture is collectively trained on the loss function which encourages that the input is reconstructed at the output. Hence the loss function is the mean squared error between the encoder input and the decoder output.

- The latent variable is not regularized. Picking a random latent variable will generate garbage output.

- The latent variable is deterministic values, and space lacks generative capability.

- Data compression is an essential phase in training a network. The idea is to compress the data so that the same amount of information can be represented by fewer bits.

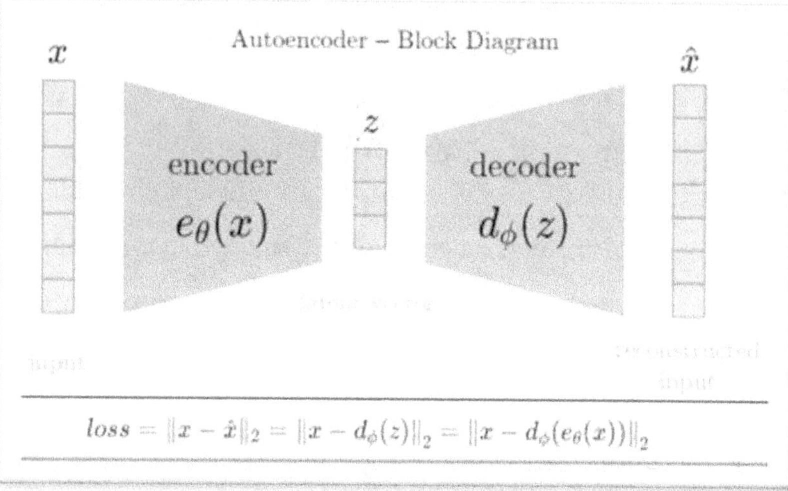


## 3.8.2 Variational Auto Encoder (VAE)

◉ Variational autoencoder addresses the issue of non-regularized latent space in autoencoder and provides the generative capability to the entire space.

◉ Instead of outputting the vectors in the latent space, the encoder of VAE outputs parameters of a pre-defined distribution in the latent space for every input.

◉ The VAE then imposes a constraint on this latent distribution forcing it to be a normal distribution.

◉ The latent variable in the compressed form is the mean and variance.

◉ The training loss of VAE is defined as the sum of the reconstruction loss and the similarity loss (the KL divergence between the unit Gaussian and decoder output distribution.

- ⊙ The latent variable is smooth and continuous i.e., random values of the latent variable generate meaningful output at the decoder, hence the latent space has generative capabilities.
- ⊙ The input of the decoder is sampled from a Gaussian with mean/variance of the output of encoder.

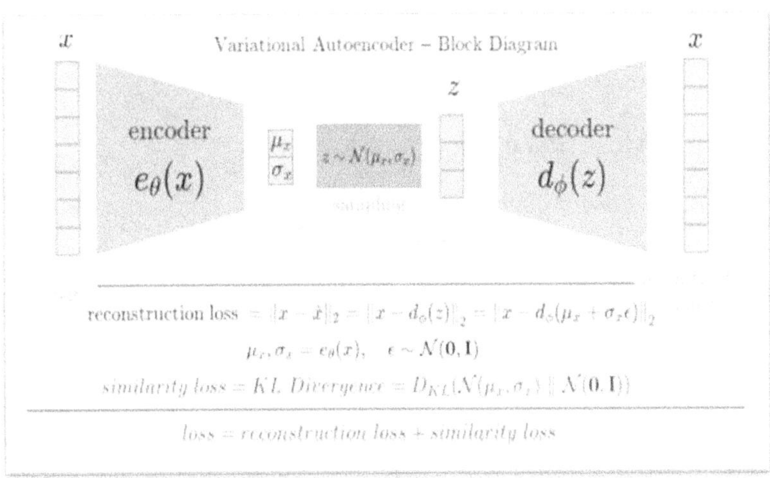


## 3.9  Most Common Loss Functions

Loss functions are crucial in machine learning, guiding models on how well they're performing by quantifying the difference between predicted and actual outcomes. The most common loss functions include Mean Squared Error (MSE), often used in regression tasks to measure the average squared difference between predicted and actual values. Cross-entropy loss, commonly applied in classification tasks, evaluates the discrepancy between predicted probabilities and the actual class labels. Other loss functions, like Hinge Loss for Support Vector Machines, focus on maximizing the margin between classes, further refining model performance.

There are many types of loss functions. These loss functions are further divided as shown below:

❑ Regression Loss Functions

- Mean Squared Error Loss
- Mean Squared Logarithmic Error Loss
- Mean Absolute Error Loss
- L1 Loss
- L2 Loss
- Huber Loss
- Pseudo Huber Loss

❑ Binary Classification Loss Functions

- Binary Cross-Entropy
- Hinge Loss
- Squared Hinge Loss

❑ Multi-class Classification Loss Functions

- Multi-class Cross Entropy Loss
- Sparse Multiclass Cross-Entropy Loss

## ▪ Kullback-Leibler Divergence Loss

| Loss Function Name | Description | Function |
| --- | --- | --- |
| Regression Losses | | |
| Mean Bias Error | Captures average bias in prediction. But is rarely used for training. | $\mathcal{L}_{MBE} = \dfrac{1}{N} \sum\limits_{i=1}^{N} (y_i - f(x_i))$ |
| Mean Absolute Error | Measures absolute average bias in prediction. Also called L1 Loss. | $\mathcal{L}_{MAE} = \dfrac{1}{N} \sum\limits_{i=1}^{N} |y_i - f(x_i)|$ |
| Mean Squared Error | Average squared distance between actual and predicted. Also called L2 Loss. | $\mathcal{L}_{MSE} = \dfrac{1}{N} \sum\limits_{i=1}^{N} (y_i - f(x_i))^2$ |
| Root Mean Squared Error | Square root of MSE. Loss and dependent variable have same units. | $\mathcal{L}_{RMSE} = \sqrt{\dfrac{1}{N} \sum\limits_{i=1}^{N} (y_i - f(x_i))^2}$ |
| Huber Loss | A combination of MSE and MAE. It is parametric loss function. | $\mathcal{L}_{Huber} = \begin{cases} \frac{1}{2}(y_i - f(x_i))^2 & |y_i - f(x_i)| \le \delta \\ \delta(|y_i - f(x_i)| - \frac{1}{2}\delta) & otherwise \end{cases}$ |
| Log Cosh Loss | Similar to Huber Loss - non-parametric. But computationally expensive. | $\mathcal{L}_{LogCosh} = \dfrac{1}{N} \sum\limits_{i=1}^{N} log(cosh(f(x_i) - y_i))$ |
| Classification Losses (Binary + Multi-class) | | |
| Binary Cross Entropy (BCE) | Loss function for binary classification tasks | $\mathcal{L}_{BCE} = \dfrac{1}{N} \sum\limits_{i=1}^{N} y_i \cdot log(p(x_i)) + (1 - y_i) \cdot log(1 - p(x_i))$ |
| Hinge Loss | Penalizes wrong and right (but less confident) predictions. Commonly used in SVMs | $\mathcal{L}_{Hinge} = max(0, 1 - (f(x) \cdot y))$ |
| Cross Entropy Loss | Extension of BCE loss to multi-class classification | $\mathcal{L}_{CE} = \dfrac{1}{N} \sum\limits_{i=1}^{N} \sum\limits_{j=1}^{M} y_{ij} \cdot log(f(x_i))$ <br> N samples M classes |
| KL Divergence | Minimizes the divergence between predicted and true probability distribution | $\mathcal{L}_{KL} = \sum\limits_{i=1}^{N} y_i \cdot log(\dfrac{y_i}{f(x_i)})$ |

## 3.10 Double Descent and Bias-Variance Trade-off

The trade-off between bias and variance in supervised learning is essential for finding a model that generalizes well. High-bias models often underfit, as they fail to capture the patterns in the data, while high variance models overfit by being too sensitive to noise. As model size increases, bias and variance are inversely proportional, meaning reducing one increases the other. The key is to find a balance between the two, leading to an optimal model size that generalizes well. In a k-NN regression example, this balance is achieved at k=7, which minimizes both underfitting and overfitting.

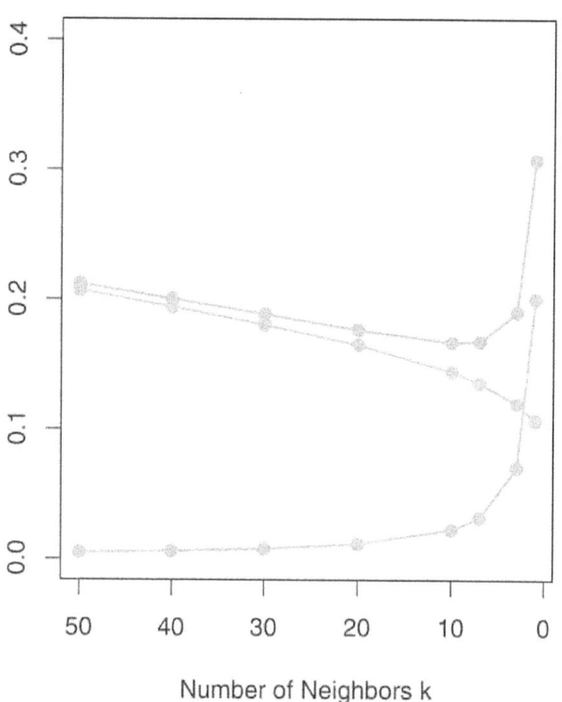



The classical bias-variance tradeoff suggests that increasing model complexity beyond a certain point harms generalization, as variance rises dramatically and further decreases in bias become less beneficial. However, recent advancements in deep neural networks challenge this idea. With improved computational technologies, state-of-the-art models are becoming increasingly complex across various domains, yet still show better performance with appropriate architectures. This trend defies traditional statistical learning expectations, where experts might find it counterintuitive that increasing complexity leads to better models, rather than overfitting. Different mechanisms drive this effect in modern AI and data science.

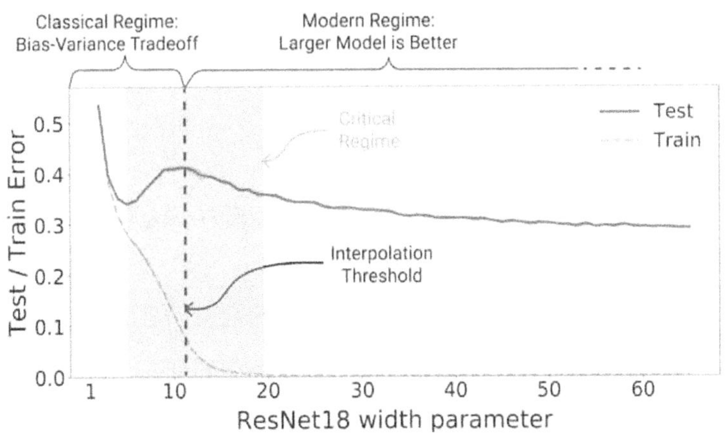


"Double descent" describes a phenomenon where increasing model complexity initially reduces testing error, followed by a rise in error after reaching a "sweet spot" suggested by classical bias-variance tradeoff. Surprisingly, when complexity surpasses the interpolation threshold, the testing error decreases again, sometimes falling below the previous minimum. This suggests that increasing complexity in deep neural networks can often improve generalization by capturing implicit patterns in the data. The exact cause of the double descent is still being explored.

An interesting analogy compares model complexity to human brain maturity: early learning resembles under-parameterization, where common patterns are recognized, while later, greater complexity allows for deeper, abstract understanding, leading to better generalization like over-parameterization in models. Though this perspective is speculative, it highlights intriguing parallels between data-driven models and human cognition.

## 3.11 Hyperparameter Tuning in Machine Learning

Hyperparameters are parameters that are set before the learning process begins and are crucial for the model's performance. Each section in the image focuses on a specific machine-learning algorithm and the key hyperparameters that should be tuned for optimal performance.

## Linear Regression

- **Regularization Parameter (Alpha)**: Adjusting this in ridge and lasso regression helps to control overfitting by penalizing large coefficients. This makes the model more robust and generalizable.

## Logistic Regression

- **The inverse of Regularization Strength (C)**: Tweaking this parameter helps in finding the balance between fitting the training data well and maintaining generalization to unseen data. A small value for C implies stronger regularization.

- **Penalty Term (L1 or L2)**: Selecting the right type of penalty helps the model focus on the most relevant features, which can improve classification accuracy.

## Decision Tree

- **Various Parameters**:
  - **max_depth**: Controls the maximum depth of the tree, preventing it from becoming too complex.
  - **min_samples_split**: The minimum number of samples required to split a node.

- **min_samples_leaf**: The minimum number of samples that can be at a leaf node.
- **criterion**: Measures the quality of a split (e.g., Gini impurity or entropy).

These parameters help prevent the model from overfitting while capturing essential patterns in the data.

❑ Support Vector Machines (SVM)

- **C**: Controls the trade-off between maximizing the margin and minimizing classification error.
- **Kernel Type**: Different kernels (linear, polynomial, RBF) transform the input space to find the optimal boundary between classes.
- **Gamma**: Defines how far the influence of a single training example reaches. A small value means far, and a large value means close.
- **Degree**: Only relevant for polynomial kernels, controls the flexibility of the decision boundary.

Proper tuning of these parameters ensures a balance between precision and efficiency.

❑ K-Nearest Neighbors (KNN)

- **n_neighbors**: The number of neighbors to consider when classifying a new point.

- **Weights**: Determines whether all points in each neighborhood are weighted equally, or closer points are weighted more.
- **Distance Metric**: Influences how distances between points are calculated, which is critical for accurate predictions in KNN.

Overall, this image highlights the importance of hyperparameter tuning in machine learning and provides a concise guide for optimizing these algorithms.

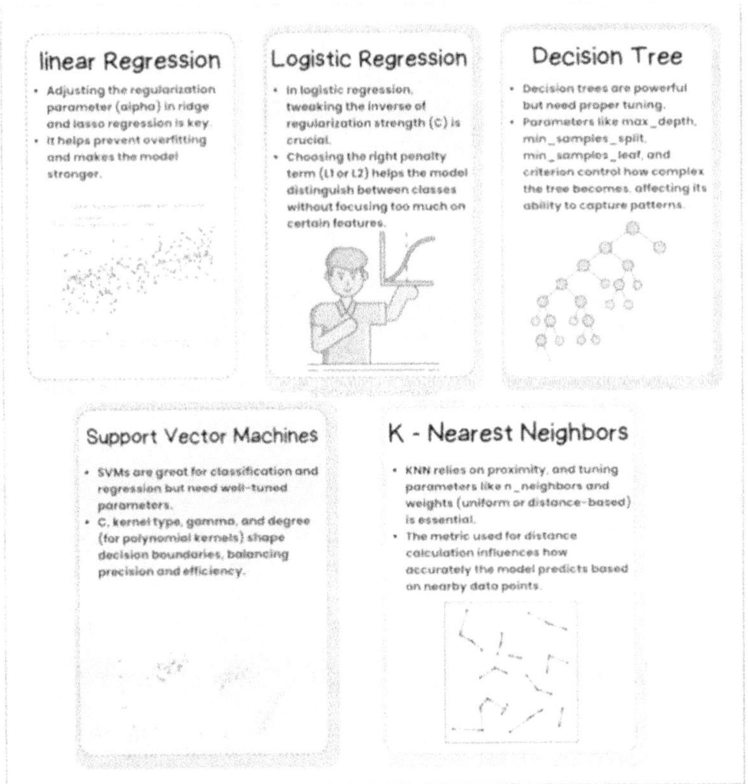

The most significant algorithms' hyperparameter adjustment in machine learning is also broken down in the graphic below.

| Representation | Algorithm Name | Hyperparameter |
| --- | --- | --- |
| | Linear Regression | Regularization parameter (alpha for Ridge/ Lasso Regression |
| | Logistic Regression | C (Inverse of regularization strength), penalty (L1, L2) |
| | Decision Tree | Max_depth, min_samples_splits, min_samples_leaf, criterion |
| | K- Nearest Neighbors | n_neighbors, weights, metric |
| | Support Vector Machines | C, Kernel, gamma, degree (for polynomial kernel) |

## 3.12 Machine Learning Model Building

The image below provides a flowchart representation of the process involved in building a machine-learning model. It outlines the key steps from the initial dataset to the evaluation of model performance.

# Data Scientist Roadmap

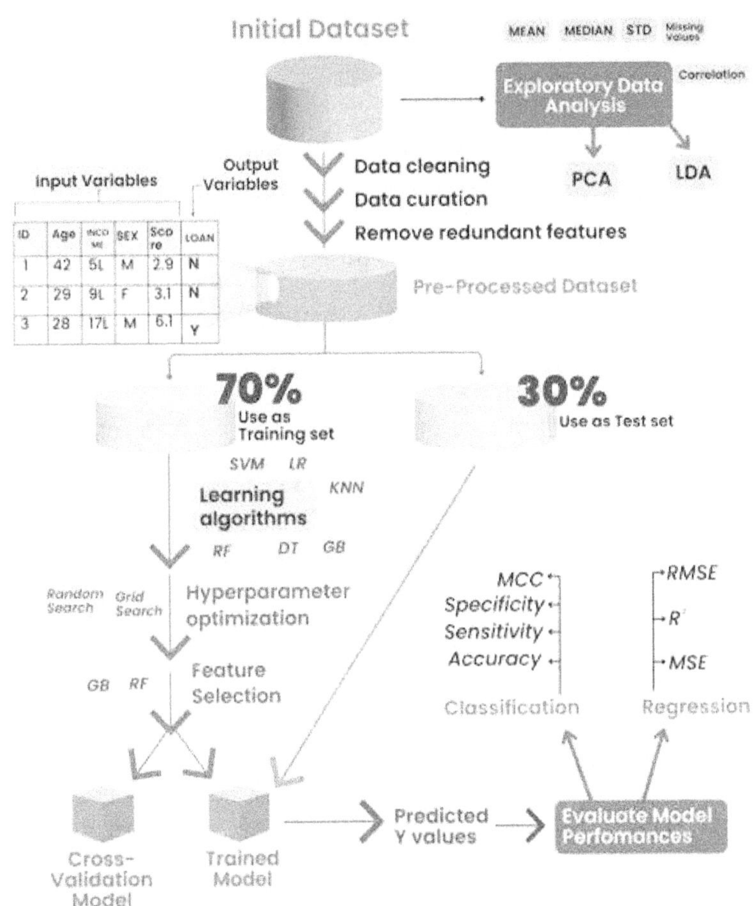






- **Input Variables (X1, X2, etc.):** These are the features or predictors in the dataset.

- **Output Variables (Y):** These are the target variables that the model is being trained to predict.

The dataset comprises multiple rows of data points with

corresponding input and output variables.

❑ Data Pre-Processing

- **Data Cleaning**: This step involves removing or correcting incorrect or incomplete data entries.

- **Data Curation**: Organizing and managing the dataset to ensure its quality.

- **Data Redundant Features**: Removing features that do not provide unique information to the model, such as duplicate or highly correlated features.

❑ Exploratory Data Analysis (EDA)

- **PCA (Principal Component Analysis)**: A dimensionality reduction technique used to simplify the dataset while preserving as much variability as possible.

- **SOM (Self-Organizing Map)**: A type of unsupervised learning used for clustering and visualizing high-dimensional data.

- **EDA** helps understand the underlying patterns and structures in the data before building the model.

❑ Data Splitting

- **70% as Training Set**: Most of the dataset is used to train the machine learning model.

- **30% as Test Set**: A smaller portion of the dataset

is reserved to evaluate the performance of the trained model on unseen data.

❑ Model Building (Training Set)

- **Learning Algorithms**: Various machine learning algorithms are applied to the training data, such as:
  - ✓ SVM (Support Vector Machines)
  - ✓ DL (Deep Learning)
  - ✓ KNN (K-Nearest Neighbors)
  - ✓ GBM (Gradient Boosting Machine)
  - ✓ RF (Random Forest)
  - ✓ DT (Decision Trees)
- **Hyperparameter Optimization**: Tuning the model's parameters to improve its performance.
- **Feature Selection**: Identifying and selecting the most relevant features for the model to improve accuracy and reduce overfitting.

❑ Prediction

The trained model generates predicted Y values (output variables) based on the input variables in the test set.

❑ Model Evaluation

- ***Classification Metrics*** (for models that classify data):
  - ✓ **MCC (Matthews Correlation Coefficient)**

- ✓ **Specificity**: True negative rate.

- ✓ **Sensitivity**: True positive rate (also known as recall).

- ✓ **Accuracy**: The overall correctness of the model.

- *Regression Metrics* (for models that predict continuous values):

  - ✓ **RMSE (Root Mean Square Error)**

  - ✓ **$R^2$ (Coefficient of Determination)**

  - ✓ **MSE (Mean Square Error)**

These metrics are used to assess the performance of the model and determine how well it is making predictions.

## ❏ Evaluate Model Performances

The final step is to evaluate the model's performance using the test set. Based on this evaluation, the model may be further refined or deployed.

# Chapter 4

# Data Analysis

## 4.1  ETL (Extract, Transfer, and Load)

ETL is a fundamental data integration process that involves extracting data from various sources, transforming it into a suitable format, and loading it into a target system, often a data warehouse.

❑ Extract

- **Source data from systems:** This stage involves gathering data from diverse sources like databases, files, APIs, or other systems.

- **Pull relevant information centrally:** Data is extracted and consolidated into a central location for further processing.

❑ Transform

- **Cleanse, restructure, and enrich data:** Data undergoes cleaning to remove inconsistencies, errors, and duplicates. It's restructured to match the target system's format and enriched with additional information if needed.

- **Standardize and align data:** Data is formatted consistently across different sources to ensure compatibility and comparability.
- Data quality and validation: Data is checked for accuracy, completeness, and adherence to predefined standards.

❑ Load

- **Transfer transformed data:** Cleansed and transformed data is moved to the target system, usually a data warehouse.
- **Load into data warehouse:** Data is loaded into the designated tables or structures within the data warehouse.
- **Full or incremental load:** You can choose to load the entire dataset (full load) or only the changes since the last load (incremental load).
- **Monitoring & maintenance:** The loaded data is monitored for errors or inconsistencies, and maintenance tasks are performed to ensure data integrity and accessibility.

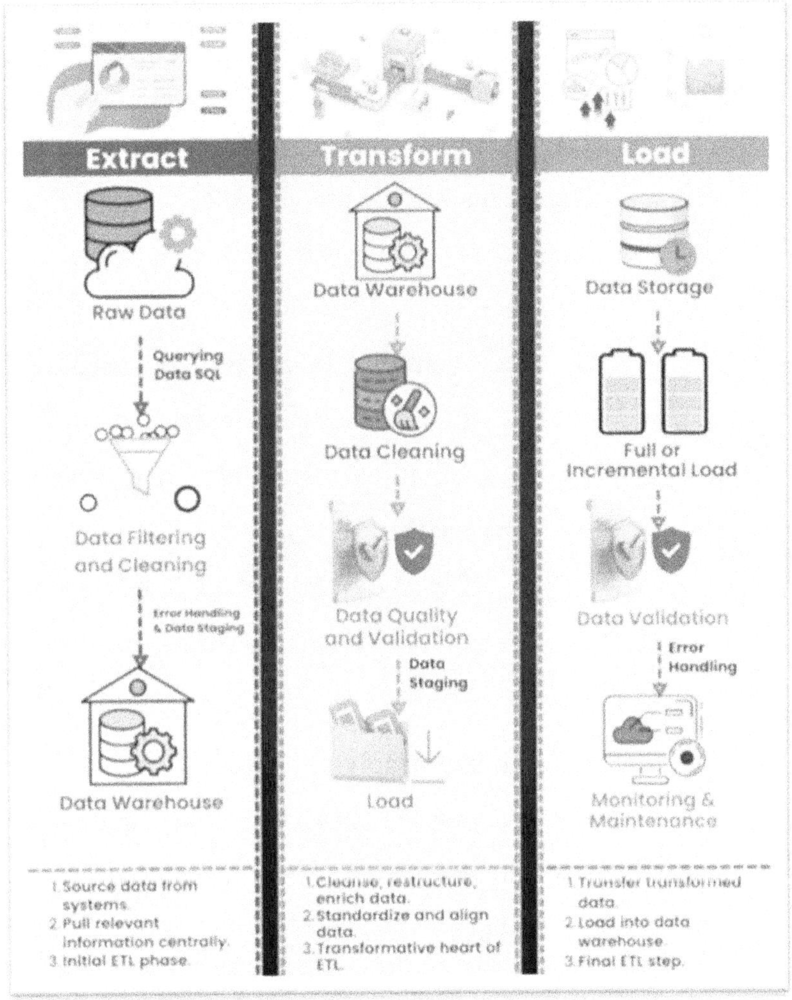


## 4.2 EDA (Exploratory Data Analysis)

EDA is a critical initial step in data analysis. It involves examining data to understand its characteristics, spot patterns, identify anomalies, and uncover potential relationships between variables. This understanding guides further analysis and decision-making.

❑ Data Distribution

- ↻ This section likely depicts histograms or density plots for numerical variables. It shows how data points are distributed across different values.
- ↻ Key insights:
    - ▪ Identify the shape of the distribution (normal, skewed, bimodal, etc.).
    - ▪ Observe central tendencies (mean, median, mode).
    - ▪ Detect outliers that might be erroneous or require further investigation.

❑ Missing Data

- ↻ This section probably visualizes missing values using heat maps or bar charts. It helps understand the extent and pattern of missing data.
- ↻ Key insights:
    - ▪ Identify variables with high missing value percentages.
    - ▪ Decide on strategies to handle missing data (imputation, removal, or analysis adjustments).

❑ Outliers

- This section typically shows box plots or scatter plots with highlighted outliers. Outliers are data points significantly different from the majority.
- Key insights:
  - Identify potential errors or anomalies in the data.
  - Consider transforming or removing outliers based on their impact and cause.

## Correlation

- This section often displays a correlation matrix or scatter plots to visualize relationships between variables.
- Key insights:
  - Identify strong positive or negative correlations between variables.
  - Assess potential multicollinearity issues in regression models.

## Patterns

- This section might include line charts, time series plots, or other visualizations to reveal trends or patterns over time or across categories.
- Key insights:

- Discover seasonal patterns, cyclical trends, or unexpected fluctuations.
- Identify potential relationships or causal effects between variables.

❑ Data Types

- This section lists the variables in the dataset along with their data types (numerical, categorical, date/time).
- Key insights:
  - Understand the nature of each variable for appropriate analysis techniques.

❑ Data Visualization

- This section might showcase examples of different visualization techniques (histograms, bar charts, scatter plots, etc.).
- Key insights:
  - Explore various ways to visualize data effectively.
  - Choose appropriate visualizations based on the data type and the insights sought.

❑ Data Quality

- This section could represent checks for data consistency, completeness, and accuracy.
- Key insights:
  - Ensure data is reliable and suitable for analysis.
  - Address data quality issues before proceeding with modeling.

***EDA serves as a crucial exploratory phase to:***

- ✓ Familiarize yourself with the data.
- ✓ Detect potential issues like outliers, missing values, and inconsistencies.
- ✓ Understand the distribution and relationships of variables.
- ✓ Generate hypotheses for further analysis.
- ✓ Inform data cleaning and preprocessing steps.
- ✓ Choose appropriate visualization and modeling techniques.

Remember, EDA is an iterative process. You might revisit different aspects of the data as you uncover new insights.

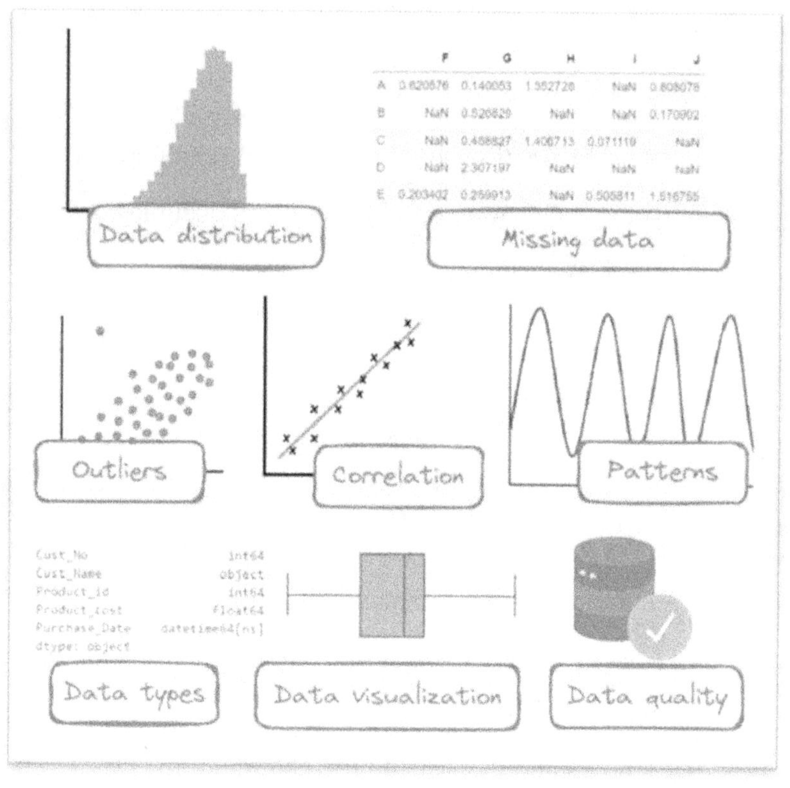


## 4.3  Data Cleaning

Data cleaning is a crucial preprocessing step in data analysis. It involves identifying and correcting errors, inconsistencies, and inaccuracies within a dataset to ensure data quality and reliability.

❑  Loading and Inspecting Data

The initial step involves loading the data into a suitable environment and conducting an initial inspection to understand its structure, format, and potential issues.

❑ Deleting Columns

Unnecessary or irrelevant columns are removed from the dataset to streamline analysis and reduce noise.

❑ Handling Duplicates

Duplicate records are identified and either removed or consolidated to maintain data integrity.

❑ Data Type Conversion

Data types are converted to appropriate formats (e.g., numerical, categorical, and date) to ensure accurate calculations and analysis.

❑ Handling Missing Data

Missing values are addressed through techniques like imputation, removal, or analysis adjustments to maintain data completeness.

❑ Dealing with Outliers

Outliers, which are data points significantly different from the rest, are identified and handled through methods like removal, capping, or transformation.

## 4.4  Outliers

Treating outliers in a dataset is crucial for accurate statistical analysis and machine learning modeling, as outliers can significantly affect the results. Here are some common strategies for handling outliers:

- **Identification** First, identify the outliers. This can be done through various methods:
    - **Visual methods**: Use box plots, scatter plots, or histograms to inspect the data for outliers visually.
    - **Statistical methods:** Employ rules based on standard deviations (e.g., values more than 3 standard deviations from the mean) or interquartile ranges (e.g., below Q1 - 1.5*IQR or above Q3 + 1.5*IQR, where Q1 and Q3 are the first and third quartiles, respectively, and IQR is the interquartile range).
- **Analysis** Once identified, analyze the outliers to determine their cause. Consider whether they result from data entry errors, measurement errors, or natural variations in the data.

## Treatment Options

After analysis, choose an appropriate method to handle them:

- **Removing**: If outliers are due to errors or are not relevant to the study, they may be removed. However, care must be taken as this can lead to loss of information.

- ⟳ **Transforming**: Apply transformations to reduce the impact of outliers. Logarithmic, square root or Box-Cox transformations are common.

- ⟳ **Imputation**: Replace outliers with more representative values, such as the mean, median, or value predicted by a model. This method should be used cautiously to not introduce bias.

- ⟳ **Capping**: Outliers are capped at a certain value. For example, values above the 99th percentile might be set to the value of the 99th percentile.

- ⟳ **Keeping**: In some cases, outliers are genuine rare events or variations that are of interest to the study. In such cases, they are kept and analyzed separately.

## ❑ Modeling With Outliers

Some machine learning algorithms are more robust to outliers than others. For example, tree-based methods are generally less sensitive to outliers than linear regression or clustering algorithms. Choosing Data Science or modifying algorithms to be more robust to outliers can be an effective strategy.

***Best Practices*** - The treatment of outliers should be informed by domain knowledge and the specific objectives of the analysis or modeling effort. - Document the identification and treatment process for transparency and reproducibility. - Be cautious of over-manipulating data, which can lead to bias or loss of valuable information. Properly handling outliers is a balance between improving your model's performance and maintaining the integrity and representativeness of your data. Outlier detection refers to the process of identifying data points that deviate significantly from most of the data, suggesting a different mechanism generated them. Identifying outliers is crucial because they can affect the results of statistical analyses and models. Here's how you can identify outliers:

❑ Statistical Methods

- **Z-Score:** Data points with a Z-score (the number of standard deviations from the mean) beyond a certain threshold (e.g., 3 or -3) are considered outliers. o

- **IQR (Interquartile Range) Method:** Data points lying below Q1 - 1.5IQR or above Q3 + 1.5IQR (where Q1 and Q3 are the first and third quartiles, respectively) are outliers.

❑ Visualization

- **Box Plots:** Visualize the distribution of the data and identify outliers as points that fall outside of the whiskers.

* **Scatter Plots:** Help in visually spotting outliers by showing data points that fall far away from the cluster of other data points.

❑ Machine Learning Methods

Algorithms like Isolation Forest, DBSCAN, and Local Outlier Factor (LOF) can automatically detect outliers in complex datasets.

Choosing the right method depends on the nature of the data and the context of the analysis. It's also important to investigate the cause of outliers before deciding to remove or adjust them, as they can sometimes be valuable for understanding the dataset better.

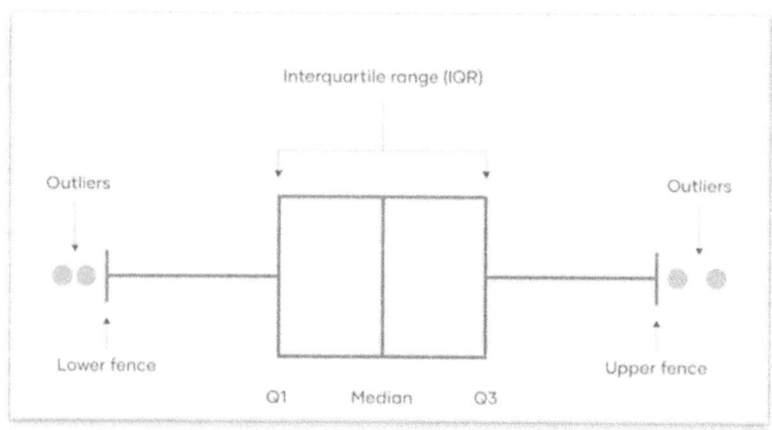


## 4.4.1 Anomalies and Outliers

In data analysis and machine learning, an anomaly refers to an observation that deviates from the expected pattern of a dataset. Anomalies are often subtle deviations rather than drastic outliers, and they can indicate underlying changes in the data. For example, in a bank's transaction system, international purchases might follow the same general spending pattern (e.g., groceries, hotels) but occur in non-native countries. This difference in location would qualify as an anomaly rather than an outlier, as it still conforms to the spending behavior but differs in one specific feature location. Anomalies are important because they often signal a change in underlying variables that, when investigated, can reveal valuable insights. For instance, in the case of stolen credit cards, anomalies like unexpected international transactions may trigger an alert, prompting further investigation. Machine learning models need to be trained to detect such anomalies, as they represent potential areas for concern or intervention. Anomalies may not always indicate a problem but could reflect variations in the process that require attention and understanding for accurate decision-making.

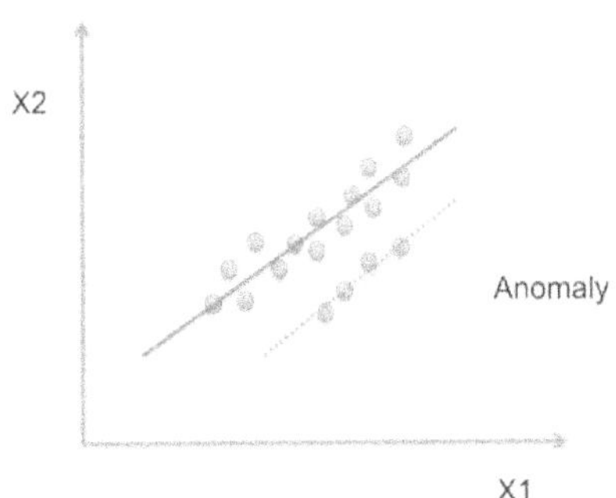

An outlier, as defined in statistics, is an observation that is significantly distant from the median, either on the higher or lower end. Unlike anomalies, which often signal changes in underlying variables, outliers may not always have a clear explanation and could result from random chance, measurement errors, or complex variable interactions.

In data science and machine learning, outliers can distort measures of central tendency (like the mean) and dispersion (like variance). Identifying and understanding outliers is crucial because they can impact the accuracy of models and analyses. Various methods are used to detect outliers, ranging from simple visual tools such as box plots and histograms to more complex mathematical approaches that measure deviation from the mean.

The decision to include or exclude outliers in the dataset depends on the context. Some outliers may be valuable data points that reveal important insights, while others might be erroneous and skew the analysis. Determining their relevance requires careful evaluation, which is often the subject of further investigation in data analysis.

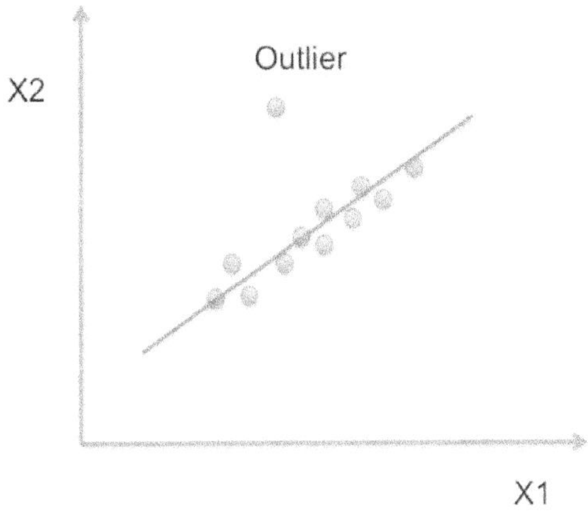


## 4.4.2 Isolation Forest Algorithm

The isolation forest algorithm detects anomalies using a tree-based approach by isolating instances within a dataset. It models normal data and identifies anomalies as being few and distinct in the feature space. The algorithm creates a random forest by generating decision trees at random, where features and threshold values are randomly chosen at each node to split the dataset. The process continues until all instances are isolated.

Anomalies, being distant from other data points, tend to be isolated in fewer steps than normal instances on average across all trees. This enables the algorithm to effectively identify anomalies.

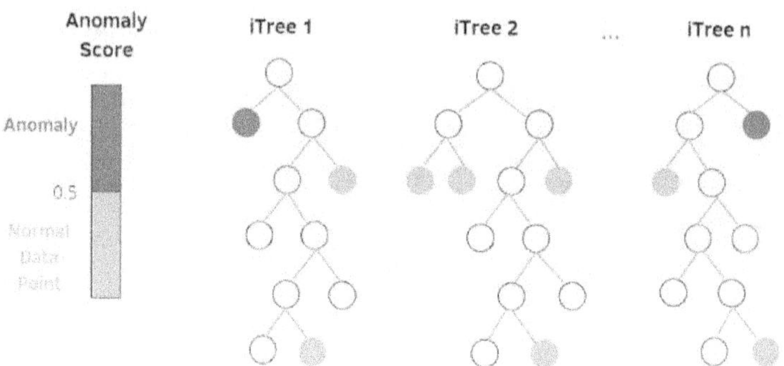


## 4.4.3 Cook's Distance

Cook's distance calculates the impact that every data point (row or observation) has on the expected result. To determine the extent to which an observation has an impact on the fitted values, the cook's distance for each observation 'i' calculates the change in $\hat{Y}$ (fitted Y) for all observations, both with and without the observation 'i'. To determine how much the projected values of all other observations change, you construct a model both with and without the observation "i" in the dataset.

$$D_i = \frac{\sum_{j=1}^{n} \left( \hat{Y}_j - \hat{Y}_{j(i)} \right)^2}{p \times MSE}$$

*Where,*

- $\hat{Y}j$ is the value of the jth fitted response when all the observations are included.

- $\hat{Y}j(i)$ is the value of the jth fitted response, where the fit does not include observation i.

- MSE: the mean squared error.

- p is the number of coefficients in the regression model.

**Pros:**

- Considers all variables in the model when calling out influential points.

- Formula-based, intuitive to understand.

**Cons:**

- To compute Cook's distance of each row requires the model to be retrained. So, it is computationally expensive to apply this method to other algorithms besides linear regression.

## 4.4.4  Quartiles and Interquartile Range (IQR)

An illustration of the Interquartile Range (IQR) in a normally distributed dataset would produce a perfectly symmetrical box plot. This symmetry is unique to normal distributions, and most real-world box and whisker plots won't look like this.

The concept of quartiles is quite simple. In a sorted numeric dataset, the median represents the middle value. Quartiles, on the other hand, divide the data into four equal parts. Quartile 1 (Q1) marks the 25th percentile, Quartile 3 (Q3) marks the 75th percentile, and Quartile 2 (Q2) is simply the median or the 50th percentile. Mathematically, these positions are calculated as follows:

For a dataset of size n:

- If n is odd, we use (n+1). If n is even, we simply use n.
- The formulas for the positions of the quartiles are:

*Position of Q1 = (n+1)/4*

*Position of Q2 = 2(n+1)/4*

*Position of Q3 = 3(n+1)/4*

**Example:**

Given the dataset: 4, 7, 7, 9, 11, 13, 17, 23, 31, 39, 666, with n = 11:

- *Q*1 is at position 3, so Q1 = 7
- Q2 is at position 6, so Q2 = 13
- Q3 is at position 9, so Q3 = 31

If the calculated position isn't an exact whole number, choose the value closest to the median.

Next, the Interquartile Range (IQR) is simply the distance between Q1 and Q3, calculated by:

*IQR = Q3 - Q1*

This range contains the middle 50% of the data, while the

remaining 25% of the values lie on either side of the IQR.

Box and whisker plots visualize these quartiles, showing which values fall within the "normal" range (within the whiskers) and which are considered outliers (outside the whiskers).

To determine the whiskers' boundaries, use the following formulas:

- Lower Whisker: Q1 - (1.5 × IQR)
- Upper Whisker: Q3 + (1.5 × IQR)

Values that fall beyond these whiskers are regarded as outliers because they are statistically rare, given the overall distribution of the dataset.

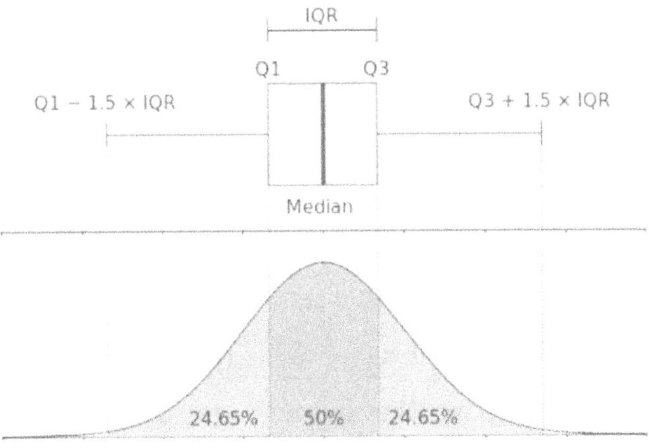


## 4.4.5 Local Outlier Factor

One technique for identifying outlier observations is the local outlier factor. There are four types of outlier detection methods: density, clustering, dispersion, and depth. Outliers can be defined using LOF using density-based scoring. The KNN (nearest neighbor search) algorithm is comparable to it. The distinction is that in KNN, we are looking for observations that are closely related to each other, whereas in LOF, we are looking for observations that are dissimilar from each other. The local outlier factor algorithm consists of four components:

- K-Distance and K-Neighbors
- Reachability Distance
- Local Reachability Density
- Local Outlier Factor Calculation

❑ K-Distance and K-Neighbors

To measure the distance between observations in a dataset, we choose a hyperparameter **k** (the number of neighbors). For instance, if **k=5**, the algorithm calculates the distance to the fifth nearest neighbor. A small **k** makes the algorithm sensitive to noise, while a large **k** may overlook local anomalies.

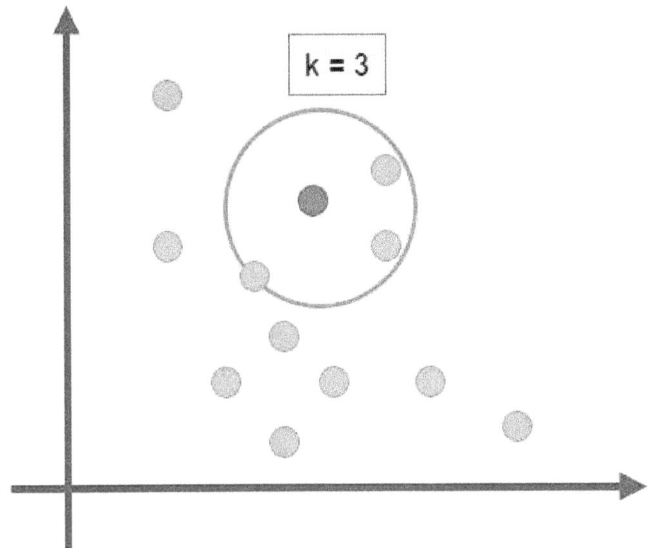



## K-Distance (LOF)

K-distance is the distance to the k-th nearest neighbor of a point.

## Reachability Distance

This is the maximum of the distance between two points and the k-distance of the second point. The distance between the two points could be calculated using Euclidean, Manhattan, or other distance measures. Reachability_Distance (a, b) = max{k-distance(b), distance (a, b)}

## Local Reachability Density (LRD)

**This** measures how densely packed the neighbors of a

point are. It is calculated by summing the reachability distances to all **k** closest neighbors of a point **a** and dividing by **k**. The inverse of this value gives the local reachability density.

$$LRD(a) = \frac{1}{\frac{1}{k}\sum_{n \in N_k(a)} \text{Reachability Distance}(a,n)}$$

Where:

- $a$ is the data point for which we are calculating the LRD.

- $N_k(a)$ represents the set of the $k$-nearest neighbors of point $a$.

- Reachability Distance$(a, n)$ is the reachability distance betw

## ❏ Local Outlier Factor (LOF)

LOF compares the local reachability density of a point **a** to the densities of its **k** nearest neighbors. The densities of these neighbors are summed, divided by the density of **a**, and then divided by **k**.

$$LOF(a) = \frac{\frac{1}{k}\sum_{n \in N_k(a)} LRD(n)}{LRD(a)}$$

Where:

- $N_k(a)$ is the set of $k$-nearest neighbors of point $a$.
- $LRD(n)$ is the Local Reachability Density of a neighbor $n$.
- $LRD(a)$ is the Local Reachability Density of point $a$.
- $k$ is the number of nearest neighbors considered.

## 4.4.6 Euclidean Distance

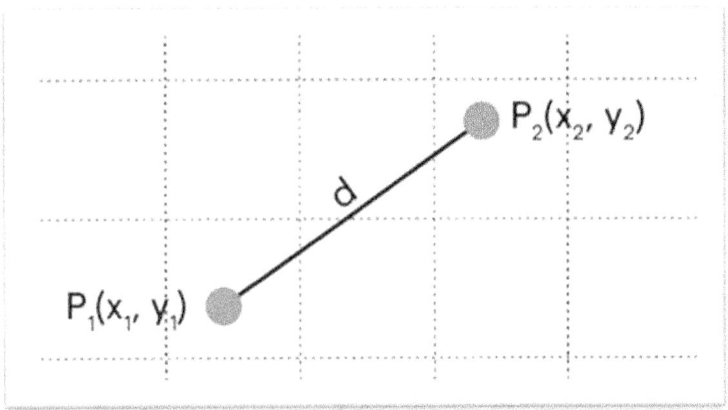


Euclidean Distance is the straight-line distance between two points in space, named after the Greek mathematician Euclid. It's widely used in fields like mathematics, physics, and computer science.

In 2D space, the distance between two points P1(x1, y1) and P2(x2,y2) is calculated using the formula:

$$d = \sqrt{(x2 - x1)^2 + (y2 - y1)^2}$$

In 3D space, the formula expands to:

$$d = \sqrt{(x2 - x1)^2 + (y2 - y1)^2 + (z2 - z1)^2}$$

❑ Examples and Applications

- **Optimization problems:** Finding the shortest route for a truck between two points.

- **Space science:** Calculating the distance between stars.

- **Marketing segmentation:** Comparing shopping patterns between customers.

- **Image recognition:** Measuring the color difference between pixels.

- **Movie recommendations:** Comparing rating patterns between movies.

- **Healthcare diagnostics:** Measuring differences in medical test results.

- **Social network analysis:** Studying the connectivity between nodes in a network graph.

## 4.4.7 Mahalanobis Distance

Mahalanobis distance is a statistical measure used to determine the similarity between two data points in a multidimensional space. It is instrumental in data analysis, pattern recognition, and classification tasks. This distance metric considers the covariance structure of the data, which makes it suitable for situations where the variables are correlated.

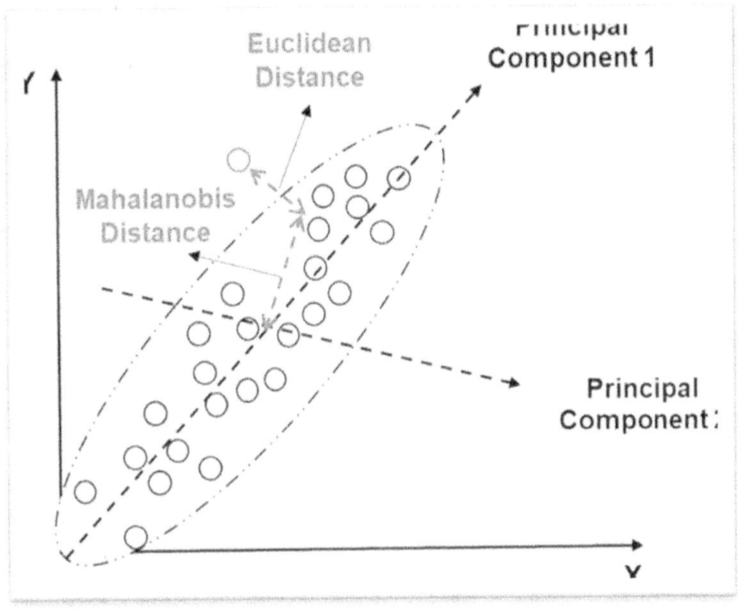


To determine the distance between data points, the Mahalanobis distance formula considers the dataset's covariance matrix and mean vector. The data is standardized, creating an environment with unit variances and uncorrelated variables.

In a multidimensional space, the number of standard deviations that are one data point from the dataset mean is calculated using the Mahalanobis distance formula. The following is the formula:

$(D) = \sqrt{((X - \mu)' \Sigma^{-1} (X - \mu))}$

Where:

- **D** is the Mahalanobis distance between the two data

points.

- **X** represents the vector of values for the data point one wants to measure the distance.

- **μ (mu)** is the mean vector of the multivariate dataset, containing the mean values of each variable.

- **Σ (Sigma)** is the covariance matrix of the dataset, which captures the relationships and variances between variables.

- **Σ^ (-1)** is the inverse of the covariance matrix.

## 4.4.8  Mahalanobis Distance vs Euclidean Distance

Below is a comparison between Mahalanobis distance and Euclidean distance:

| Aspect | Mahalanobis Distance | Euclidean Distance |
|---|---|---|
| *Definition and Formula* | Measures dissimilarity while considering the covariance structure of the data. It is calculated using the mean vector, covariance matrix, and data point vector. | Measures the straight-line distance between two data points in a multidimensional space. It is calculated as the square root of |

| Aspect | Mahalanobis Distance | Euclidean Distance |
|---|---|---|
| | | the sum of squared differences along each dimension. |
| *Sensitivity to Data Distribution* | Assumes that the data follows a multivariate normal distribution. | Assumes no specific data distribution; it is applicable to a wide range of data types and distributions. |
| *Robustness to Scaling* | Scale-invariant; it is not affected by the scaling of variables. | Sensitive to outliers, extreme values can significantly affect distance calculations. |
| *Handling Correlated Variables* | Suitable for datasets with correlated variables; considers variable correlations in the covariance matrix. | Treats variables independently; does not account for correlations between variables. |

| Aspect | Mahalanobis Distance | Euclidean Distance |
| --- | --- | --- |
| *Dimensionality* | Becomes less effective with high-dimensional data due to increased computational complexity and potential data sparsity. | Generally applicable to high-dimensional data, although interpretation can become challenging as dimensions increase. |
| *Outlier Sensitivity* | May be less sensitive to outliers due to covariance structure consideration. | It may be less sensitive to outliers due to covariance structure consideration. |
| *Customization of Thresholds* | Customizable thresholds can be set to identify outliers or anomalies, providing flexibility. | Thresholds are typically not customized, and outliers are identified based on distance magnitude alone. |

| Aspect | Mahalanobis Distance | Euclidean Distance |
| --- | --- | --- |
| *Applications* | Widely used in various fields, including finance, healthcare, quality control, and image recognition, where correlations between variables are important. | Commonly applied in geometric and spatial analysis, machine learning, and data clustering tasks when correlations between variables are less critical. |

## 4.4.9 Minimum Covariance Determinant (MCD) Method

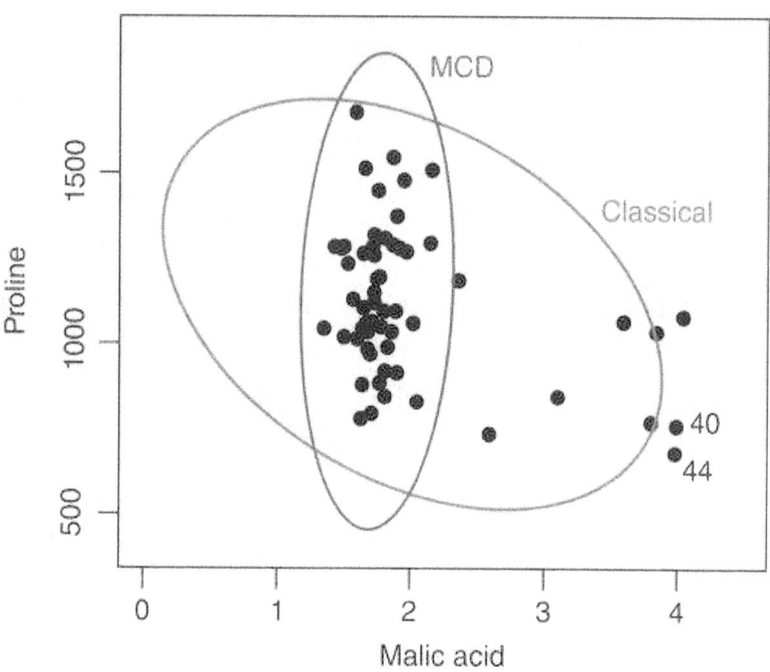


When working with data, we assume it follows a certain probability distribution, and points with low probability density are recognized as anomalies. For elliptically distributed data (like Gaussian), this can be done by calculating the Mahalanobis distance, which measures the distance from each point to the mean (center of mass) divided by the ellipsoid's width in that direction. Anomalies are identified as points with a Mahalanobis distance greater than a certain threshold.

## ❑ Covariance Matrix

The covariance matrix is a square matrix that represents the variance of the components of a data vector along its diagonal and the covariances between the components in the off-diagonal elements.

## ❑ Estimation Challenge

When working with raw data, we don't have the true mean and covariance matrix, so they must be estimated. Anomalies can distort these estimates, pulling the mean toward outliers and inflating the covariance matrix, making anomalies less noticeable.

## ❑ MCD Method (Minimum Covariance Determinant)

MCD is Another robust version of Mahalanobis, a method to estimate the mean and covariance matrix in a way that minimizes the influence of anomalies. It does this by selecting a subset of the data that is free of anomalies. From this subset, the mean and covariance matrix are calculated. The subset with the smallest determinant of the covariance matrix (indicating a tight, dense distribution) is chosen, which helps exclude anomalies from the estimation.

Mahalanobis Distance is not a robust way to determine

outliers, as it uses the means and covariances of all the data – including the outliers – to determine individual difference scores.

Minimum Covariance Determinant MCD calculates the mean and covariance matrix based on the most central subset of the data (by default, 66%), before computing the Mahalanobis Distance. This is deemed to be a more robust method of identifying and removing outliers than regular Mahalanobis distance.

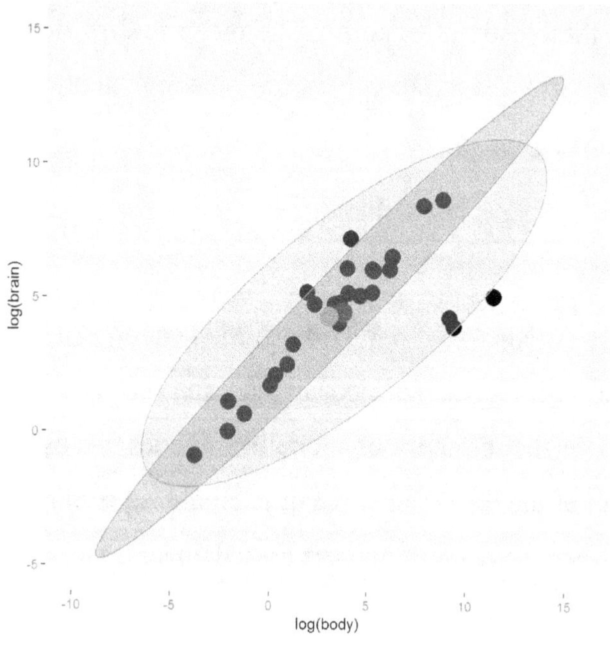


## 4.4.10  Single-Class SVM

One-class SVM, a variant of Support Vector Machines,

specializes in anomaly detection, primarily used in unsupervised learning tasks. This algorithm identifies outliers by training on a single class of data, making it ideal for spotting anomalies in complex datasets, such as fraud detection or unusual patterns in medical imaging.

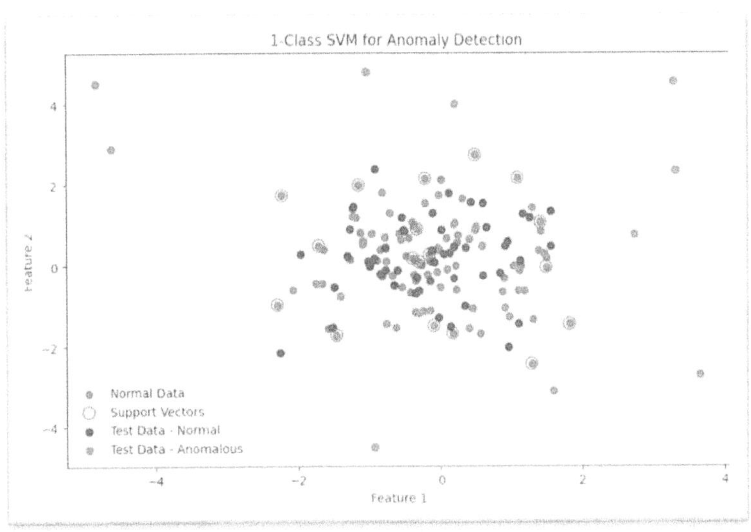


## 4.5  Handling Missing Values

Handling missing data in a dataset involves several strategies, depending on the nature of the data and the extent of the missing values. Here are common methods:

❏ Deletion

- **Listwise deletion**: Remove entire records where any data is missing.

- **Pairwise deletion**: Use available data while ignoring missing values during statistical analysis.

❑ Imputation

- **Mean/Median/Mode substitution**: Replace missing values with the mean, median, or mode of the column.

- **Predictive models**: Use statistical models (e.g., regression, k-nearest neighbors) to predict and fill in missing values based on other data.

- **Hot-deck imputation:** Replace a missing value with an observed response from a similar unit.

❑ Using Algorithms that Support Missing Values: Some machine learning algorithms can handle missing data directly.

❑ Assign a Unique Category: For categorical data, treat missing values as a separate category.

The choice of method depends on the analysis goals, data type, and missingness mechanism—whether it's missing completely at random (MCAR), missing at random (MAR), or missing not at random (MNAR).

## ❑ Coding missing values

These condition variables can be used to create a new variable from two other variables, a true variable, and a false variable. The result variable for an observation will take the value of the true variable when the condition variable for that observation is true. Otherwise, the observations will take the value from the false variable for that observation.

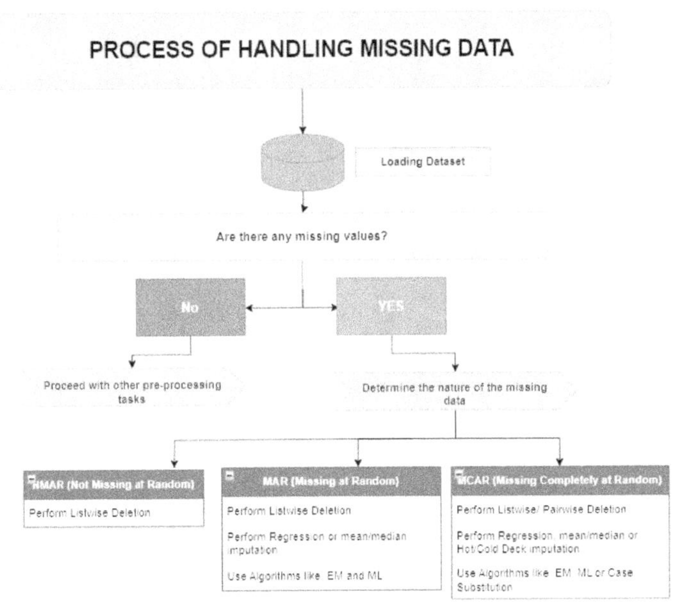


## 4.6  Balanced and Imbalanced Data

❑ **Balanced Dataset:** To illustrate, let's use a small example whereby the positive numbers in our data collection are roughly equal to the negative values. We may therefore state that our dataset is balanced. Think of the colors orange and blue as representing positive and negative values, respectively. We can conclude that there are roughly equal numbers of positive and negative values.

☐ **imbalanced dataset:** is one in which the difference between the positive and negative numbers is quite large. Subsequently, we can state that our dataset is imbalanced.

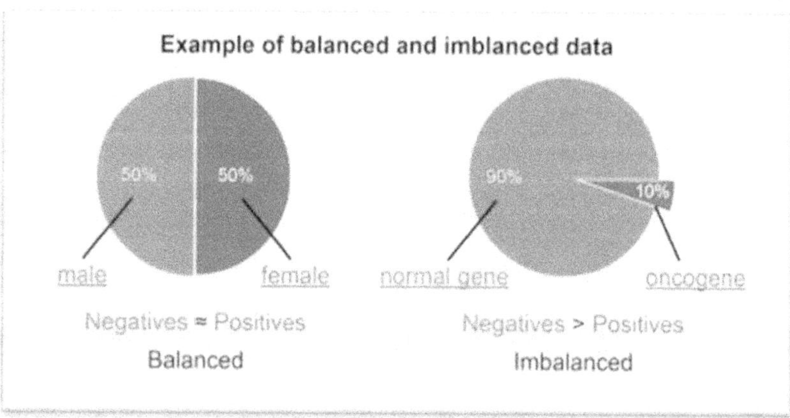


☐ dealing with the imbalance dataset

■ **Informed undersampling:** Using algorithms such as k-nearest neighbor classifier to accomplish undersampling. Conversely, one-sided selection (OSS) employs a heuristic that uses Tomek linkages to exclude noisy samples to first clean the dataset. Next, each sample is subjected to a 1-nearest-neighbor classifier application.

- **synthetic minority oversampling technique (SMOTE):** To balance the dataset, this technique attempts to generate new artificial samples of the minority class. It is a widely used approach that generates new samples based on the spatial distance between existing samples through an unsupervised algorithm. The Adaptive Synthetic Sampling method is a more advanced technique (ADASYN). This approach uses interpolation to create new samples as well, but it mostly concentrates on creating samples next to the original samples that a k-Nearest Neighbors classifier incorrectly identified.

- **Combination of over- and undersampling:** Oversampling to create artificial samples of the minor class and undersampling to remove noisy samples from the resultant space constitute a well-rounded strategy. SMOTE is used for the oversampling step and edited nearest-neighbors (SMOTEENN) or Tomek's link (SMOTETomek) can be used for the cleaning.

- **Ensemble methods:** An unsupervised approach called EasyEnsemble uses arbitrary subsets of the majority class. To generate an ensemble dataset, the original set is undersampled at random. BalanceCascade is a supervised method that successively generates balance and removes unnecessary samples in the majority class to construct a final classifier. It is another comprehensive approach. In contrast to the previous approach, this one makes use of a classifier to guarantee that the incorrectly categorized samples can be chosen once more for the following subset.

- **Cost-sensitive methods:** To reduce the overall cost, you can consider the cost of misclassification rather than altering the dataset. You can train specific ML algorithms as cost-sensitive classifiers by employing this technique. Decision trees that take cost into account are a popular method. These are traditional decision trees with thresholds set to produce the ROC curve's most prominent point. This algorithm has some good Python implementations available as part of the University of Luxembourg's COSTCLA project.

- **Kernel and Active Learning methods:** These approaches are not easily implemented, and most of the work is theoretical with little empirical support. Active

Learning is a semi-supervised machine learning technology that has gained popularity in recent years. To collect new data points, the algorithm asks the user or an information source question. While this is an intriguing tactic, it has only been used with dense word disambiguation (DWD) datasets that are over- or under-sampled.

# Chapter 5

# Programming Foundations

## 5.1 Variables

There are different types of variables commonly encountered in data analysis and machine learning. Here's a breakdown:

- **Independent Variable:**

Variables (x1, x2) that are used as inputs in a model to predict the outcome (dependent variable y).

- **Dependent Variable:**

The output variable (y) that the model is trying to predict is based on independent variables.

- **Interaction Variables:**

This shows how the interaction between different variables (e.g., Population and Income) creates combinations that can influence the outcome.

- **Latent Variable:**

Variables that are not directly observed but inferred from other observed variables. These are unobserved variables that influence the data.

- **Confounding Variable:**

A variable (e.g., Temperature) that affects both the independent variable (Ice Cream Sales) and the dependent variable (Air Conditioner Sales), potentially leading to misleading interpretations of causal relationships.

⊙ **Control Variable:**

A variable that is held constant to isolate the true causal effect between other variables. Here, controlling Temperature allows an understanding of the true causal relationship between Ice Cream Sales and Air Conditioner Sales.

⊙ **Correlated Variables:**

Variables that change together in a similar pattern over time, such as the correlation between Air Conditioner Sales and Ice Cream Sales.

⊙ **Leaky Variable:**

A variable whose value depends on the outcome. This can introduce data leakage, where information from the outcome contaminates the input features, leading to unrealistic model performance during training.

⊙ **Non-stationary Variable:**

A variable whose statistical properties (e.g., mean, variance) change over time, making modeling more challenging.

⊙ **Stationary Variable:**

A variable with statistical properties that remain constant over time, making it easier to model.

⊙ **Lagged Variable:**

A variable that includes past values of itself or other variables to predict the current value. For example, using the previous value of x1 (lagged by one-time step) as an input.

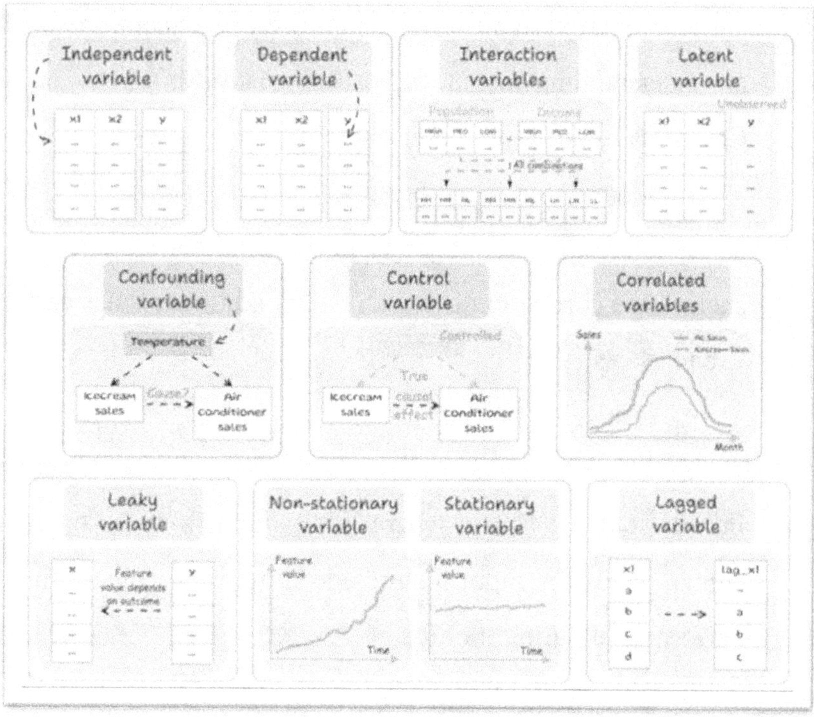

## 5.2  Data Types

There is data everywhere. Over 40 zettabytes, or 40 trillion gigabytes, of data exist in the world today, Moreover, despite its abundance, it is still so valuable that it serves as the basis for every industry, including transportation and healthcare.

## 5.2.1  Data Types According to Their Value

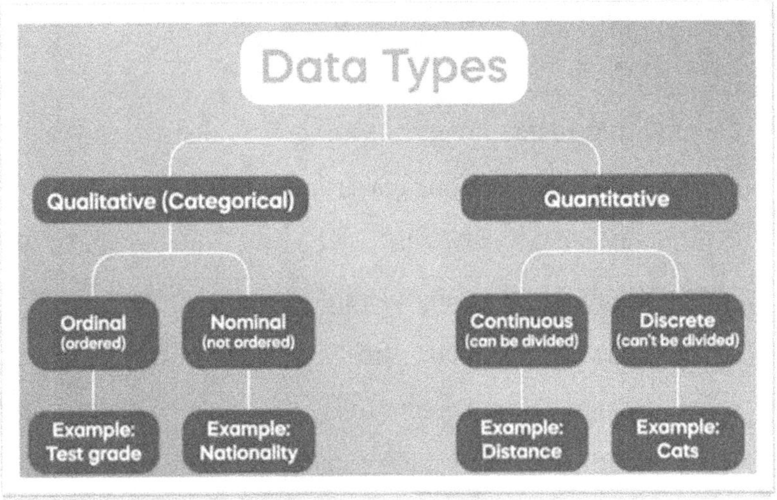


❑ Qualitative (Categorical) Data

Qualitative data often provides an item or set of items description. Because you may assign a label to a set of objects or data points, as the name suggests, it is often referred to as categorical data. Places and colors are a few examples.

Following that, two further categories of qualitative data are identified: "ordinal" and "nominal."

❑ Ordinal Data

Ordinal data, such as exam scores, economic standing, or military rank, are arranged in a certain order or ranking.

❑ Nominal Data

Unlike ordinal data, however, nominal data is not arranged in a particular order. Think of things like colors, work position, gender, and city.

❑ Quantitative (Numerical) Data

Quantitative data involves numeric values and can be categorized into continuous or discrete types.

Continuous data, like weight, can be divided into smaller units and still maintain meaningful values.

In contrast, discrete data, such as the number of kids in a school, cannot be meaningfully split into smaller parts. Differentiating between these data types can be challenging at first, but with practice, it becomes clearer.

## 5.2.2  Data Types According to Sensitivity

Data sensitivity is crucial for data professionals, as mishandling it can have serious legal consequences. Data is categorized into four levels of sensitivity:

❑ *Low Sensitivity:* Public data accessible without risk, such as website content, blogs, and company information.

❑ *Medium Sensitivity:* Internal data that, if disclosed, could cause mild harm, like donor information, emails, and personnel records.

❑ *High Sensitivity:* Confidential data, such as passwords and financial details, whose exposure could lead to significant harm to individuals and institutions.

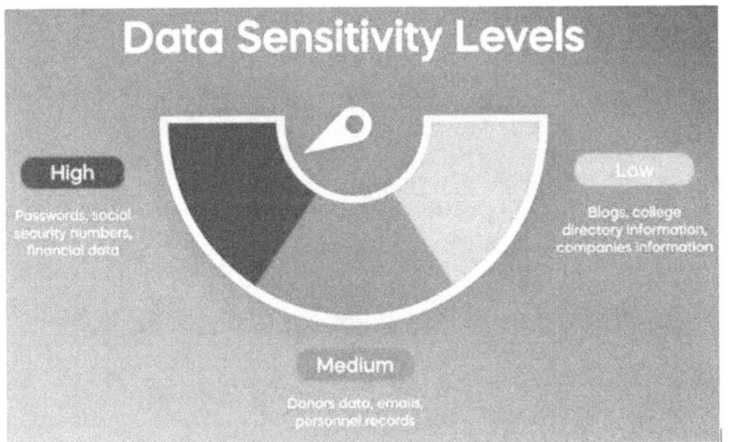


## 5.2.3  Data Types in Python

In Python, data types are essential for managing and analyzing data. The key types you'll often work with include:

☐ *Numbers:*

- Int: Whole numbers, e.g., 1, -2.

- Float: Decimal numbers, e.g., 15.2, -80.5.

- Complex: Numbers with real and imaginary parts, e.g., 9+5j.

☐ *String*: Text data, e.g., "country", "zip code".

☐ *List:* An ordered, modifiable group of values, e.g., [5, 10, "orange"].

☐ *Tuple:* Like a list, but immutable, e.g., (10, 30, "book").

- ❑ ***Set:*** An unordered group of unique values, e.g., {10, 15, 50}.
- ❑ ***Dictionary:*** Key-value pairs, e.g., {"Name": "Mary", "Age": 30}.
- ❑ ***DateTime:*** Represents date and time, e.g., 2020-05-29 15:30:22.
- ❑ ***Boolean:*** True/false values, e.g., True or False.

## 5.2.4  Importance of Data Types

Here are the reasons why understanding data types is crucial.

- ◉ Knowing the exact data format and size helps save time and space.
- ◉ It reduces the likelihood of errors in the cleaning and analysis stages.
- ◉ Ensures that the functions you'll write later will give you the desired results.
- ◉ And it helps with instrumentation, which is the process of tracking data and sending it to other systems. To instrument data properly and create an effective tracking plan, you must determine all data types beforehand.

## 5.3  Data Concepts

❑ Data Warehouse

A data warehouse is a centralized repository that stores large volumes of structured data from various external sources. The data undergoes an ETL (Extract, Transform, Load) process, where it is extracted from external sources, transformed into a suitable format, and then loaded into the data warehouse. The data warehouse serves as a primary storage area for data that can be used for data mining, reporting, and analysis. Data marts, which are smaller, focused subsets of the data warehouse, can be created to serve specific business needs.

## ❑ Data Mart

A data mart is a specialized, smaller subset of a data warehouse. It is designed to focus on a specific business line or team, providing tailored data that meets the specific needs of that group. Data marts are created from the data warehouse and are used to make data more accessible and manageable for specific departments or functions.

## ❑ Data Lake

A data lake is a vast pool of raw, unstructured data stored in its native format until it is needed. Unlike a data warehouse, a data lake can handle large volumes of varied data types, such as structured, semi-structured, and unstructured data. The flexibility and scalability of a data lake make it ideal for storing big data. Data is stored in raw format and transformed only when needed for specific purposes.

## ❑ Data Pipeline

A data pipeline refers to the series of processes involved in moving data from one system to another. This typically includes extracting data from external sources, transforming it into the required format, and loading it into a target system or storage area. Data pipelines are crucial for ensuring the smooth flow of data across different stages and systems in an organization.

## ❑ Data Quality

Data quality refers to the degree to which data meets the expectations of accuracy, validity, completeness, and consistency required by an organization. Data quality processes involve cleansing and standardizing data to ensure that it is reliable and fit for use. High data quality is essential for making informed decisions and achieving accurate insights.

## ❑ Data Mining

Data mining is the process of analyzing large datasets to uncover hidden patterns, trends, correlations, and anomalies. Data mining applications use various techniques to sift through vast amounts of data, extracting valuable information that can inform decision-making. This process often involves querying databases, analyzing metadata, and presenting results through a front-end application for easy interpretation. These concepts are fundamental to managing and processing data in modern organizations, enabling the extraction of valuable insights and supporting data-driven decision-making.

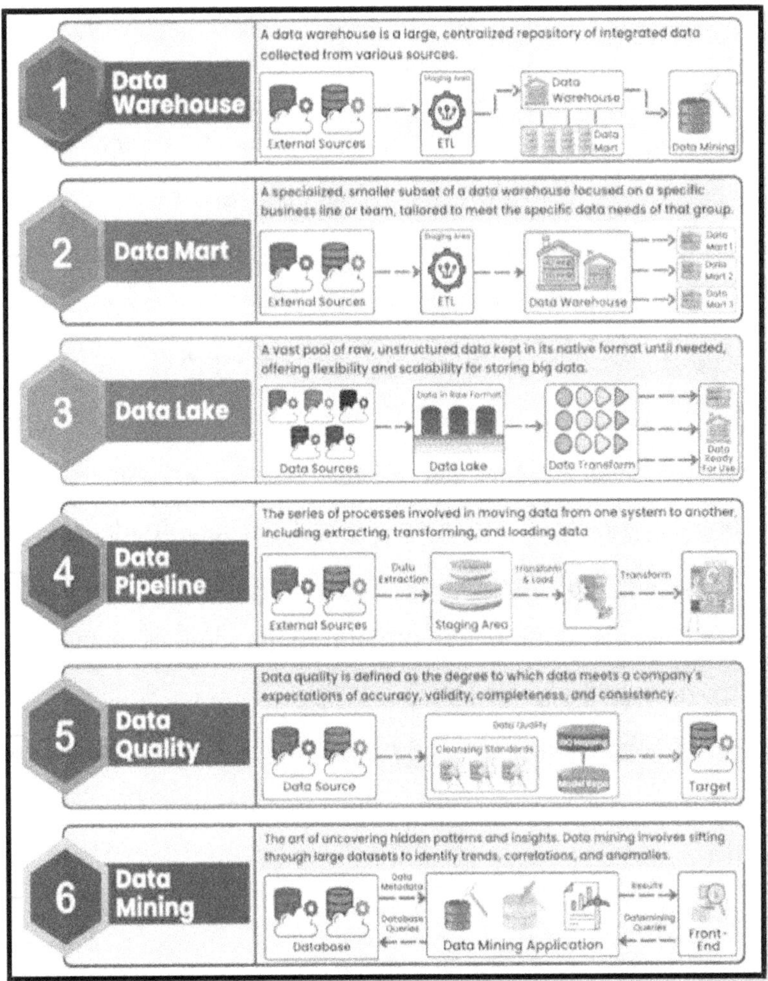

## 5.4 Loops

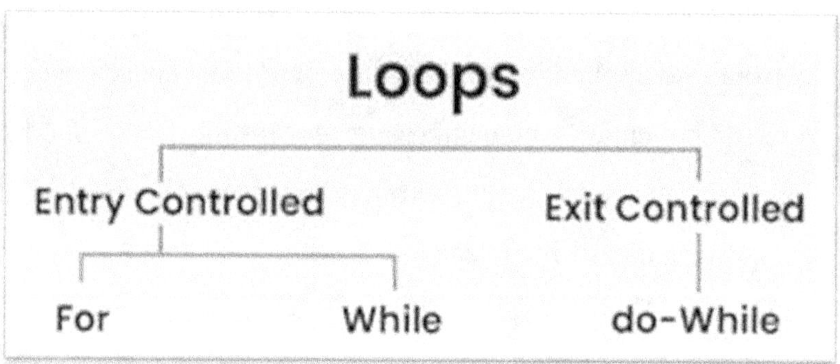


Iterations or Loops In programming, statements come in handy when we need to do a particular task repeatedly. They are crucial because they cut hours of labor down to seconds.

Loops, also known as iterative statements, are used when we need to execute a block of code repetitively. Loops in programming are control flow structures that enable the repeated execution of a set of instructions or code blocks as long as a specified condition is met. Loops are fundamental to the concept of iteration in programming, enhancing code efficiency, readability and promoting the reuse of code logic.

**Programming Loop Types**

Entry-controlled loops and exit-controlled loops are the two primary forms of loops in programming, which are distinguished by their control mechanisms.

***Entry-Controlled loops***

Before entering the loop's main body, the test condition is

verified in entry-controlled loops. Entry-controlled loops are those seen in the While and For loops.

***Exit-Controlled loops.***

In Exit controlled loops the test condition is evaluated at the end of the loop body. The loop body will execute at least once, irrespective of whether the condition is true or false. Do-while Loop is an example of Exit Controlled loop.

## 5.4.1  For Loop

For loop in programming is a control flow structure that iterates over a sequence of elements, such as a range of numbers, items in a list, or characters in a string. The loop is entry-controlled because it determines the number of iterations before entering the loop.

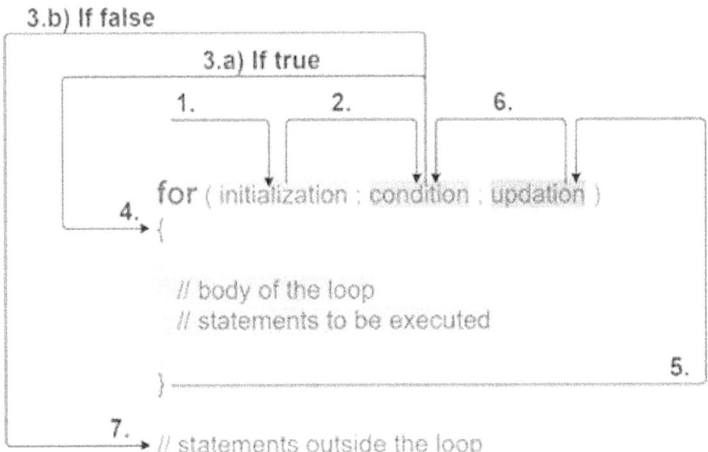

## 5.4.2  While Loop

A while loop in programming is an entry-controlled control flow structure that repeatedly executes a block of code if a specified condition is true. The loop continues to iterate while the condition remains true, and it terminates once the condition evaluates to false.

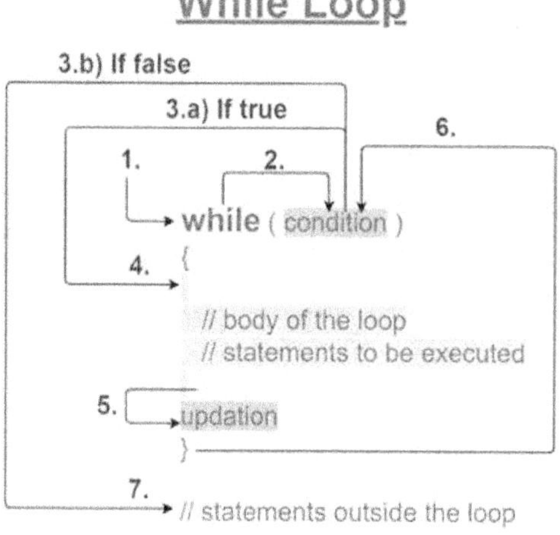



## 5.5  Functions

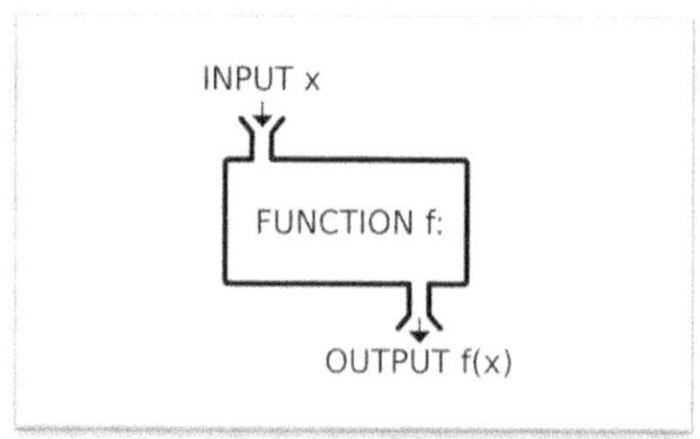



Programming functions are modular units of code created to

carry out tasks. They allow for code organization and reuse because they encapsulate a series of instructions. This article will cover the fundamentals of function, its significance, many function kinds, etc.

In programming, a function is a block of code that contains a single task or a set of related activities. Functions can return a value, have parameters, and are specified by their names. Functions are primarily designed to take a large program and divide it into smaller, easier-to-manage parts, or functions, each of which carries out a particular duty.

❏ Functions are essential in programming for several reasons

- **Modularity:** Functions break programs into smaller, manageable modules, making development, testing, and debugging easier.

- **Abstraction:** Functions hide implementation details, allowing programmers to focus on higher-level operations without worrying about complexities.

- **Code Reusability:** Functions promote code reuse, reducing redundancy by allowing the same code to be called multiple times from different parts of the program.

- **Readability and Maintainability:** Functions improve

code structure, enhancing readability and simplifying maintenance, especially in complex projects.

- **Testing and Debugging:** Functions make it easier to test and debug specific parts of the code by isolating functionality.

## ❏ Tips for Functions in Programming

- **Infinite Recursion:** Without a proper base case, recursive functions can lead to infinite recursion, so always define a base case.

- **Proper Use of Return Statements:** Ensure that all code paths in a function that should return a value do so.

- **Avoid Global Variables:** Functions should ideally rely on their input parameters and not on external variables.

- **Single Responsibility Principle:** Each function should do one thing and do it well.

### 5.6  Data Structures

The basic building blocks of computer programming are known as data structures. They specify how information is arranged, saved, and used by software. It is crucial to comprehend data structures to create algorithms that are both successful and efficient.

The most widely used data structures, including arrays, linked lists, stacks, queues, trees, and graphs, will be covered in this course.

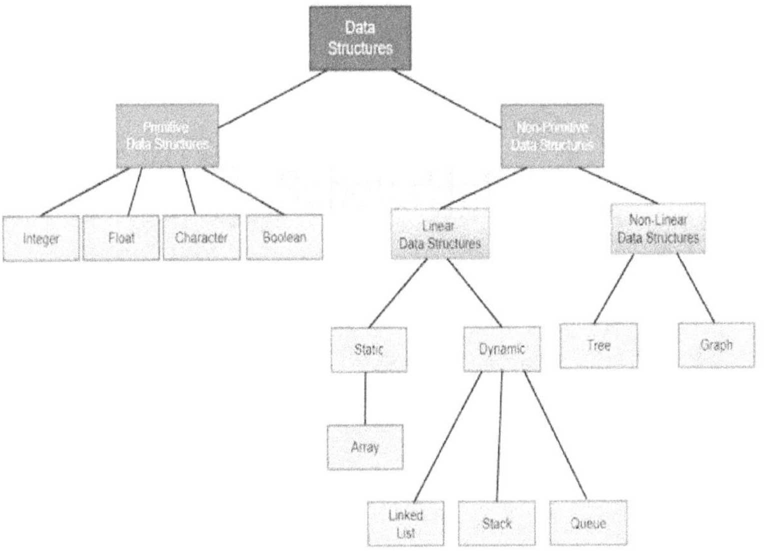


❏ Array

- Ordered collection of elements.
- The position of each element is defined by the index.
- The elements can be accessed in any order.

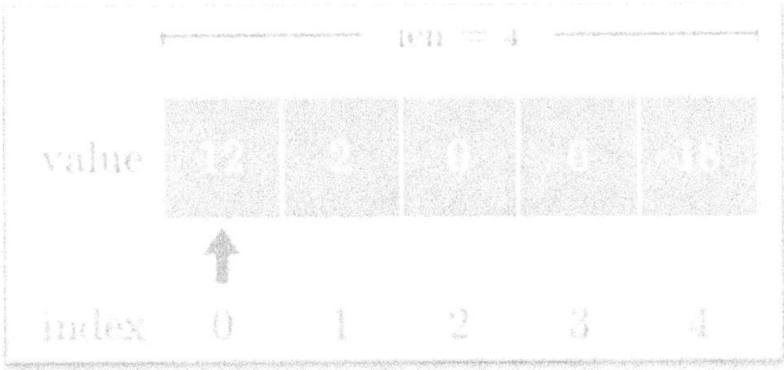

## ❑ Linked List

- Linked List do not have their order defined by their physical placement in the memory.
- Contiguous elements of the linked list are not placed adjacent to each other in the memory.
- Each linked list element contains both the values and the address (pointer) to the next linked list element.
- Hence the linked list can only be traversed sequentially going through each element at a time.

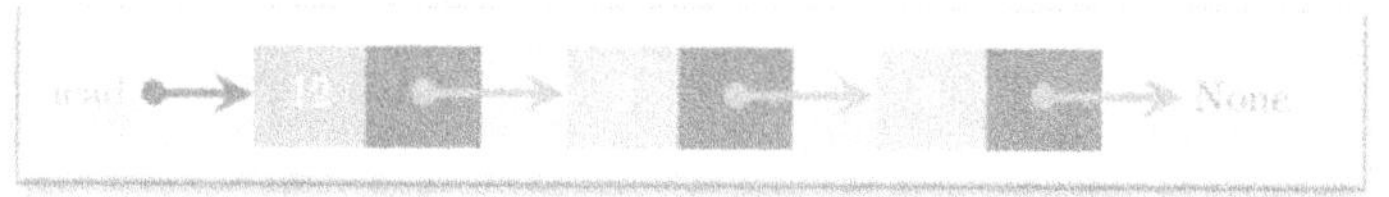

## ❑ Stack

- Stack is a sequential data structure that maintains the order of elements as they are inserted.
- Last In First Out (LIFO) order, which means that the elements can only be accessed in the reverse order as they were inserted into the stack.
- The element to be inserted last will be the first to get removed from the stack.
- Push () adds an element at the head of the stack, while pop () removes an element from the head of

the stack • A real-life example of a stack is a stack of kitchen plates.

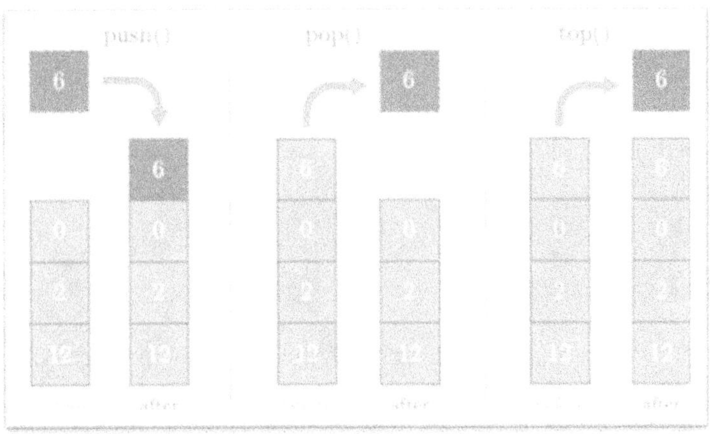

## Queue

- A queue is a sequential data structure that maintains the order of elements as they are inserted.

- First In First Out (FIFO), the element to be inserted first, will be the first to get removed from the queue.

- Whenever an element is added (Enqueue ()) it is added to the end of the queue. On the other hand, element removal (Dequeue ()) is done from the front of the queue.

- A real-life example is a check-out line at a grocery store.

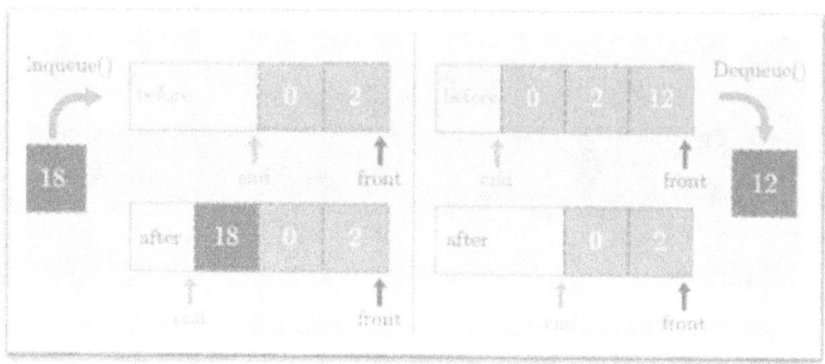

## ❏ Hash-table

- Creates paired assignments (key mapped to values) so the pairs can be accessed in constant time.
- For each (key, value) pair, the key is passed through a hash function to create a unique physical address to store the value in the memory.
- The hash function can end up generating the same physical address for different keys. This is called a collision.

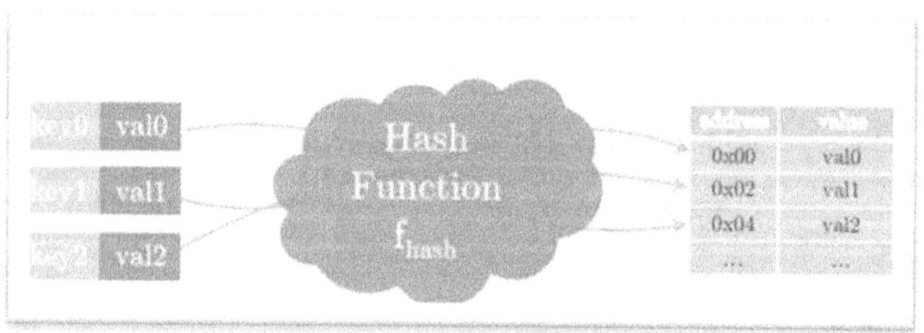


## ❏ Tree

- Maintains a hierarchical relation between its elements.
- Root Node – The node at the top of the tree.
- Parent Node – Any node that has at least one child.
- Child Node – The successor of a parent node is known as a child node. A node can be both a parent and a child node. The root is never a child node.
- Leaf Node– The node with no child node.
- Traversing – Passing through the nodes in a certain order, e.g. BFS, DFS.

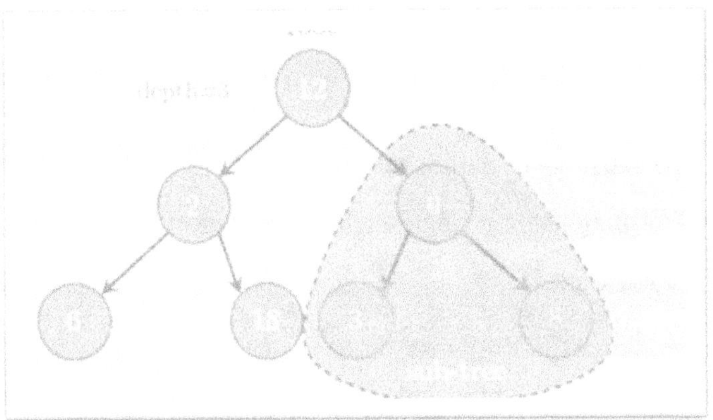

## ❏ Graph

- A graph is a pair of sets (V, E), where V is the set of all the vertices, and E is the set of all edges.
- A neighbor of a node is a set of all vertices connected with that node through an edge.

- As opposed to trees, a graph can be cyclic, which means starting from a node and following the edges, you can end up on the same node.

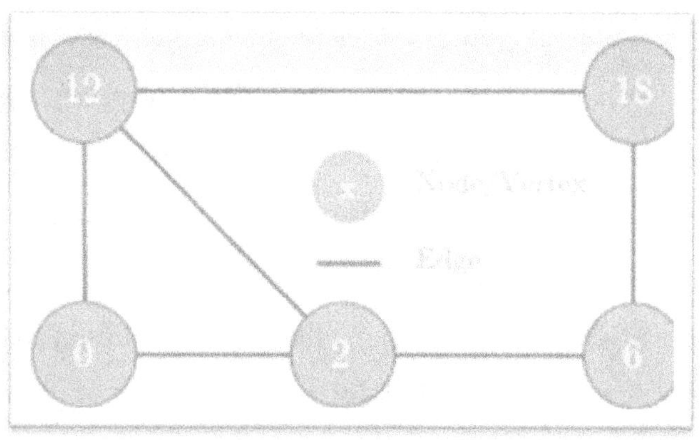


## 5.7  Types of Databases

A database is a structured set of data that is gathered and analyzed using a database management system, which is software that communicates with applications, end users, and the database itself.

- **Spatial:** Databases optimized for handling geographic data, such as locations, shapes, and spatial relationships.

    - Examples: postGIS, MongoDB Spatial

- **Blockchain:** Distributed databases that use cryptographic techniques to ensure security and transparency.

- ◔ Examples: BigchainDB, IBM Blockchain

☐ **Distributed:** Databases spread across multiple nodes for scalability and fault tolerance.

- ◔ Examples: Apache Cassandra, Amazon DynamoDB

☐ **In-memory:** Databases that store data in main memory for extremely fast access.

- ◔ Examples: Redis, Memcached

☐ **NoSQL:** Non-relational databases designed for handling large volumes of unstructured or semi-structured data.

- ◔ Examples: MongoDB, Cassandra

☐ **Relational:** Traditional databases that store data in tables with rows and columns.

- ◔ Examples: MySQL, PostgreSQL

☐ **Object-Oriented:** Databases that store data as objects with attributes and methods.

- ◔ Examples: db4o, Object DB

☐ **Graph:** Databases that store data as nodes and relationships between them.

- ◔ Examples: Neo4j, Amazon Neptune

☐ **Time-series:** Databases optimized for handling time-stamped data.

⊃ Examples: InfluxDB, Prometheus.

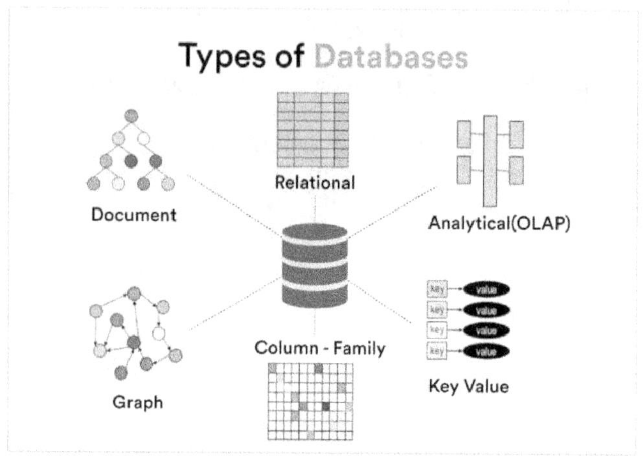


## 5.8  Algorithms

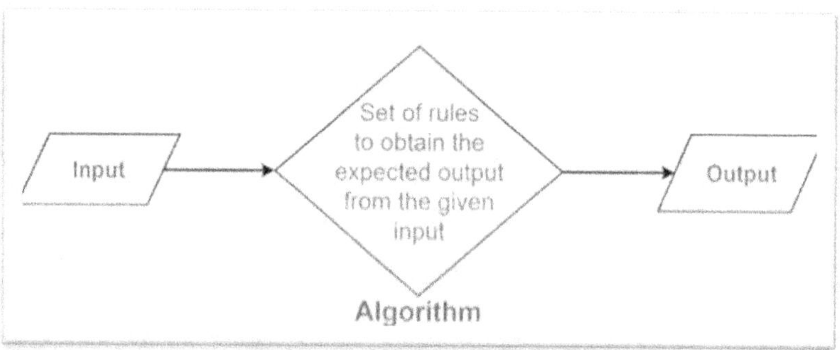


"A set of finite rules or instructions to be followed in calculations or other problem-solving operations" is the definition of the word algorithm.

Alternatively, "A finite-step mathematical problem-solving procedure that often incorporates recursive operations."

❑ Use of the Algorithms

Algorithms play a crucial role in various fields and have many applications. Some of the key areas where algorithms are used include:

- **Computer Science:** Algorithms form the basis of computer programming and solve problems ranging from simple sorting and searching to complex tasks such as artificial intelligence and machine learning.

- **Mathematics:** Algorithms are used to solve mathematical problems, such as finding the optimal solution to a system of linear equations or finding the shortest path in a graph.

- **Operations Research:** Algorithms are used to optimize and make transportation, logistics, and resource allocation decisions.

- **Artificial Intelligence:** Algorithms are the foundation of artificial intelligence and machine learning and are used to develop intelligent systems that can perform tasks such as image recognition, natural language processing, and decision-making.

- **Data Science:** Algorithms are used to analyze, process, and extract insights from large amounts of data in fields such as marketing, finance, and healthcare.

❑ Properties of Algorithm

- *It should terminate after a finite time.*
- *It should produce at least one output.*
- *It should take zero or more input.*
- *It should be deterministic means giving the same output for the same input case.*
- *Every step in the algorithm must be effective i.e. every step should do some work.*

## 5.9  Parallel Programming

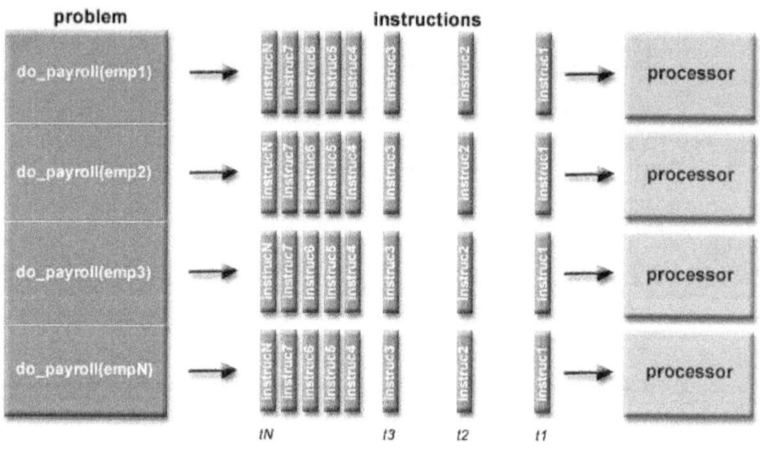


To put it simply, parallel programming is the process of breaking down an issue into smaller jobs that may be performed concurrently using numerous computing resources.

## How Does Parallel Programming Work?

Parallel programming involves breaking down tasks and distributing them across multiple processing units, such as nodes, processors, and cores, to improve performance. A node contains memory and processors, while each processor has multiple cores that execute commands. In parallel programming, developers write code to divide tasks into smaller parts that can be processed simultaneously, speeding up tasks like image recoloring by splitting the image into segments.

Parallel programming is used in a wide range of devices, from small embedded systems to supercomputers. Various programming languages, like C, C++, and Fortran, support parallelism through technologies such as OpenMP, which enables parallel tasks across cores on a single node, and MPI, which facilitates communication between nodes. While shared memory within a single node is faster, using multiple nodes allows for larger-scale processing. However, developers face challenges in effectively dividing tasks and debugging issues in their parallel applications.

## ❏ What Is Parallel Programming Used For?

Parallel programming's ability to decompose tasks makes it a suitable solution for complex problems involving large quantities of data, complex calculations, or large simulations. Previously unsolvable problems have been decomposed using parallel programming, such as weather simulations, vaccine development, and astrophysics research.

Parallel programming use cases include:

- Advanced graphics in the entertainment industry
- Applied Physics
- Climate research
- Electrical engineering
- Financial and economic modeling
- Molecular modeling
- National defense and nuclear weaponry
- Oil and gas exploration
- Quantum mechanics

## 5.10 Programming Languages

# 5.10.1 Structured Query Language (SQL)

Mastering SQL provides the tools a data analyst needs to effectively retrieve, manipulate, and analyze data, which in turn produces analyses that are more accurate and perceptive. For several reasons, a data analyst must be proficient with SQL.

- ***Data Extraction:*** To extract data from relational databases, SQL is required. To carry out your studies as a data analyst, you frequently need to access data sets from huge databases.

- ***Data Manipulation:*** SQL makes it possible to effectively filter, combine, and alter data. Once you have mastered SQL, you will be able to create sophisticated queries that support the creation of deeper analyses and insights from data.

- ***Data Integration:*** Merging information from many databases or tables is a frequent undertaking. Data integration from several sources is made feasible via SQL's JOIN and other set procedures (UNION, INTERSECT).

- ***Performance Optimization:*** An understanding of SQL optimization strategies is necessary to query huge databases effectively. Productivity may be increased, and query run times can be greatly decreased by being aware of indexes, query execution strategies, and performance tweaking.

- ***Data Cleaning:*** Accurate analysis depends on high-quality data. Strong data preparation capabilities are offered by SQL, including managing missing values, finding duplicates, and formatting correction.

- ***Reporting and Dashboarding:*** SQL databases may be integrated with a wide range of business intelligence tools and reporting platforms, including Tableau, Power BI, Looker, and Metabase. You can construct dynamic, intricate reports and dashboards by mastering SQL.

## SQL Commands:

Writing effective and optimized SQL queries can be substantially improved by having a solid understanding of how SQL queries are executed. Let's dissect it collectively now.

The logical query processing order is the sequence in which SQL query execution occurs.

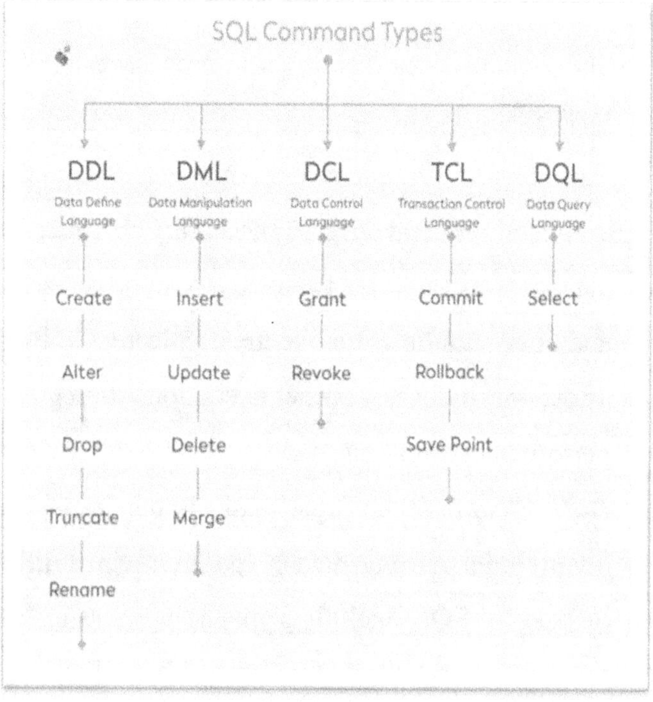

Here is a condensed list of the steps to be taken:

- **FROM**: The query's tables or views are listed in the FROM clause. It is the source of the data.

- **WHERE:** Based on predetermined criteria, the WHERE clause filters the data from the source mentioned in the FROM clause. It makes the dataset smaller.

- **GROUP BY:** The filtered data is grouped using the provided columns according to the GROUP BY clause. When aggregating data with methods like SUM, COUNT, or AVG, this step is helpful.

- **HAVING:** The HAVING clause applies conditions to filter the aggregated data. Like the WHERE clause, but for grouped data, it functions.

- **SELECT:** The columns that are included in the result set are chosen using the SELECT clause. Aggregations and expressions derived from filtered and aggregated data may be included.

- **ORDER BY:** The ORDER BY clause uses given columns or expressions to order the result set. It establishes the final row order that is returned.

- **LIMIT/OFFSET:** This optional phrase helps implement pagination or limit the number of rows returned.

Keep in mind that the physical execution order and the logical query processing order might not always coincide. The database optimizer determines the query's most effective execution method by utilizing strategies like query rewriting or parallel processing.

Understanding the logical query processing order empowers you to write optimized queries by placing conditions and aggregations strategically. It also helps interpret query results and troubleshoot performance issues.

## 5.10.2 Python

Here is a brief breakdown of the necessary tools

 **For Data Science**:

- **NumPy and Pandas** for data manipulation
- **SciPy** for scientific computing

- **Matplotlib**, **Seaborn**, **Bokeh**, **Plotly**, **and Dash** for data visualization
- **Dask** for scalable analytics

  **For Machine Learning**:

- **Scikit-Learn** for general-purpose ML
- **TensorFlow and PyTorch** for deep learning
- **Keras** for high-level neural networks
- **LightGBM**, **XGBoost**, **and CatBoost** for gradient boosting
- **Hugging Face Transformers** for state-of-the-art NLP
- **OpenAI Gym** for reinforcement learning

  **For Generative AI**:

- **GLM-PyTorch and Pyro** for probabilistic models
- **NeRF** for 3D reconstruction
- **StyleGAN** for generating realistic images.
- **JAX**, **Flax**, **DALL-E** 2, **and Imagen** for cutting-edge AI research

# Python
## Libraires and Frameworks

### Data Science

- NumPy
- Pandas
- SciPy
- Matplotlib
- Seaborn
- Bokeh
- Plotly
- Dask

### Machine learning

- Scikit-Learn
- TensorFlow
- PyTorch
- Keras
- LightGBM
- XGBoost
- CatBoost
- Hugging Face Transformers
- OpenAI Gym

### Generative AI

- GLM-PyTorch
- Pyro
- NeRF
- StyleGAN
- JAX
- Flax
- DALLE-2
- Imagen

## 5.10.3 R Programming Language

R is a programming language used for data visualization and statistical analysis. The domains of data mining, bioinformatics, and data analysis have all adopted it. Numerous extension packages that include documentation, sample data, and reusable code are added to the base R language.

R packages are collections of functions, documentation, and data that extend R's capabilities, contributing to its adoption in data science. Base packages are available immediately upon starting R, providing essential programming and statistical functions. The Comprehensive R Archive Network (CRAN), established in 1997, hosts R's source code and packages, growing to over 20,853 contributed packages by June 2024. In addition to CRAN, packages can be found on repositories like R-Forge and GitHub. R packages support a wide range of statistical techniques, and specialized projects like Bioconductor cater to genomic data analysis. One prominent example is the tidy verse package, which provides a unified interface for data manipulation, focusing on "tidy data" in data frames.

## ❑ Advantages of R language

- ➲ R is the most comprehensive statistical analysis package. As new technology and concepts often appear first in R.
- ➲ As R programming language is an open source. Thus, you can run R anywhere and at any time.
- ➲ R programming language is suitable for GNU/Linux and Windows operating systems.

- ⮑ R programming is cross-platform and runs on any operating system.
- ⮑ In R, everyone is welcome to provide new packages, bug fixes, and code enhancements.

❏ Disadvantages of R language

- ⮑ In the R programming language, the standard of some packages is less than perfect.
- ⮑ Although, R commands put little pressure on memory management. So, R programming language may consume all available memory.
- ⮑ In R basically, nobody complains if something doesn't work.
- ⮑ R programming language is much slower than other programming languages such as Python and MATLAB.

# Chapter 6

# Deep learning

Deep learning is a branch of machine learning that uses artificial neural networks (ANNs) that are architecture after the structure of the human brain.

These networks are made up of layers of connected nodes, or neurons, that process information gradually. Deep learning is superior to typical machine learning algorithms in managing complex and unstructured data, including audio, text, and images.

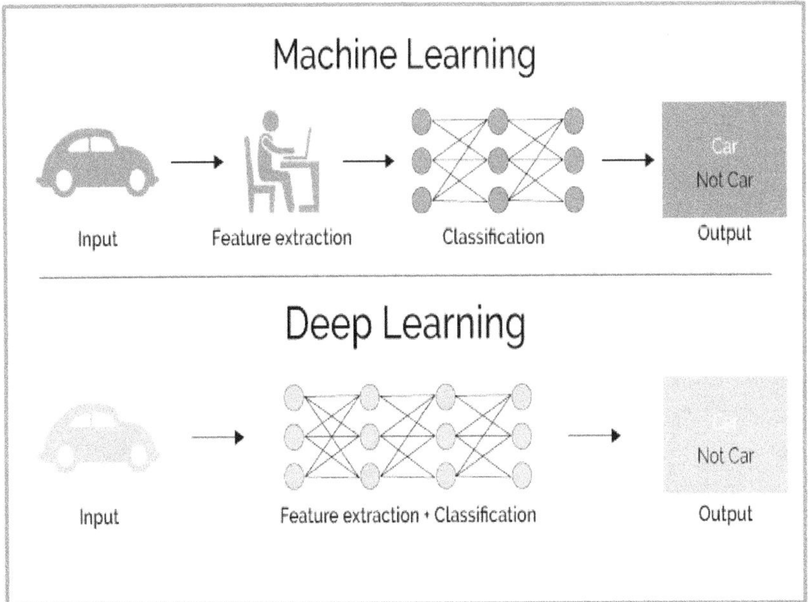

## 6.1 How Deep Learning Works

- **Data Preparation:** Collecting and organizing vast amounts of data relevant to the problem. This data is often pre-processed to extract meaningful features.

- **Neural Network Architecture:** Designing an appropriate neural network structure, considering factors like the type of data, the problem complexity, and desired output.

- **Training:** Exposing the network to the prepared data, allowing it to learn patterns and relationships through an iterative process called backpropagation.

- **Optimization:** Fine-tuning the network's parameters to improve performance using techniques like gradient descent.

- **Prediction or Classification**: Once trained, the model can make predictions or classifications on new, unseen data.

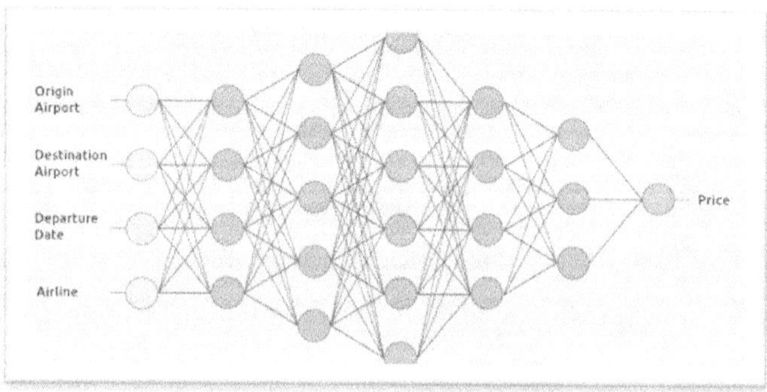

## 6.2 Types of Deep Learning Architectures

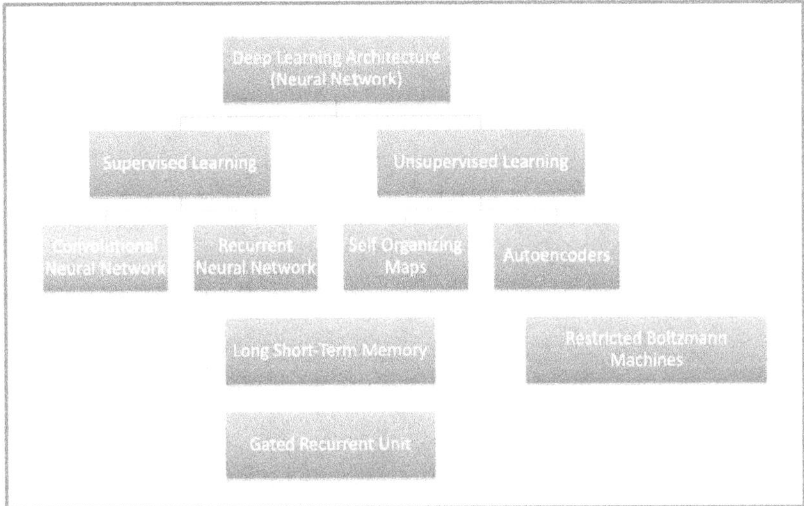


- **Convolutional Neural Networks (CNNs):** Primarily used for image and video analysis, excelling at feature extraction.

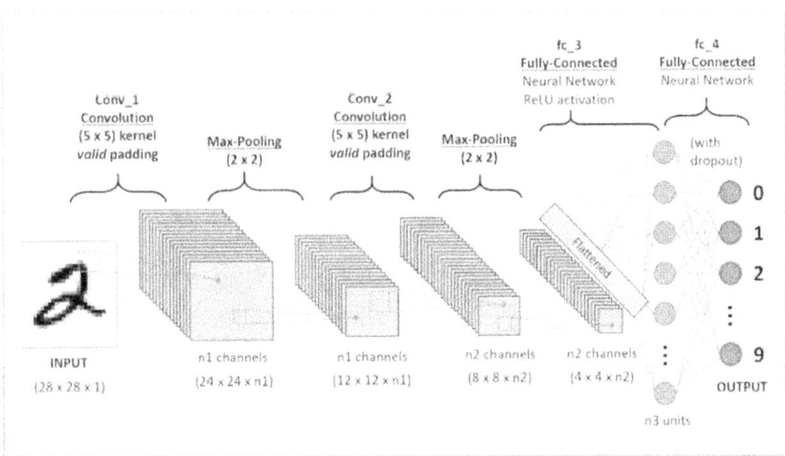

- **Recurrent Neural Networks (RNNs):** Designed to process sequential data, such as text and time series, capturing dependencies.

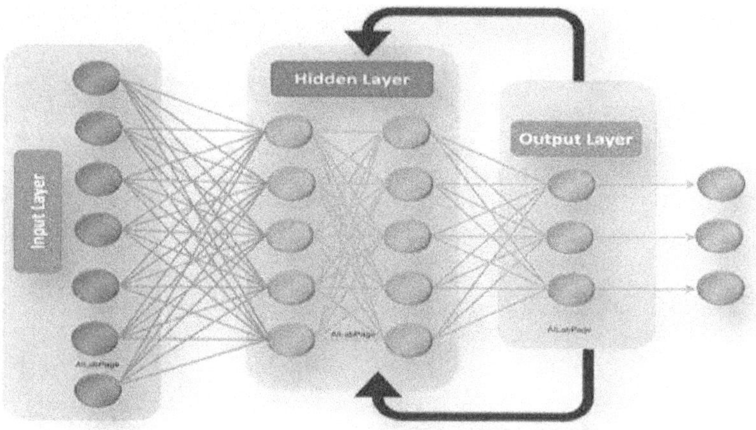


- **Long Short-Term Memory (LSTM) Networks:** A variant of RNNs addressing the vanishing gradient problem, suitable for long-term dependencies.

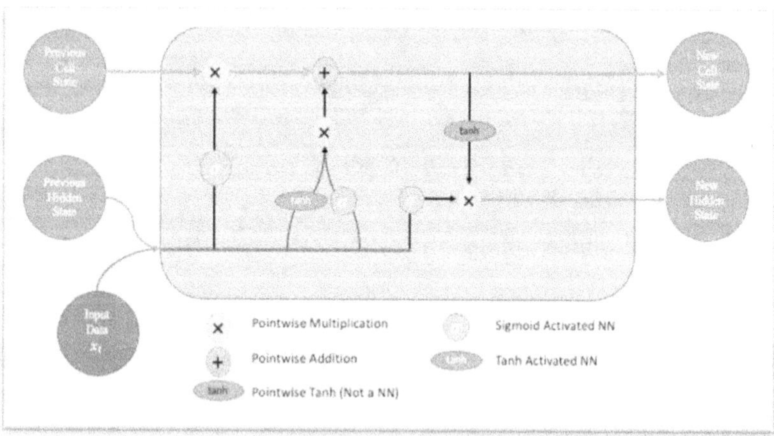

- **Generative Adversarial Networks (GANs):** Comprising a generator and discriminator, used for creating realistic synthetic data.

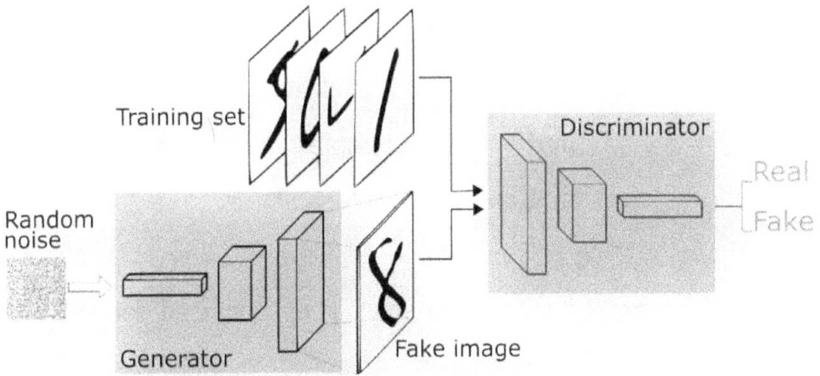


## ❑ Applications of Deep Learning

- **Computer Vision:** Image recognition, object detection, image generation.

- Natural Language Processing (NLP): Machine translation, sentiment analysis, text generation.

- **Speech Recognition:** Voice assistants, transcription services.

- **Healthcare:** Medical image analysis, drug discovery, disease prediction.

- **Autonomous Vehicles:** Object detection, path planning, decision-making.

- **Financial Services:** Fraud detection, algorithmic trading, risk assessment.

## 6.3 Deep Learning Use Cases

- **RNNs** (Recurrent Neural Networks) are effective for tasks involving sequential data, such as text, speech, and time series. Examples include chatbots, voice assistants, and weather forecasting.

- **CNNs** (Convolutional Neural Networks) excel at processing image data. They are used for tasks like image recognition, object detection, and character recognition.

- **Autoencoders** are employed for dimensionality reduction and feature extraction. They can be applied to image compression, anomaly detection, and feature extraction for other tasks.

- **GANs** (Generative Adversarial Networks) are used to generate new data like training data. Applications include generating images, music, and 3D objects, as well as tasks like image-to-emoji conversion and face attribute manipulation.

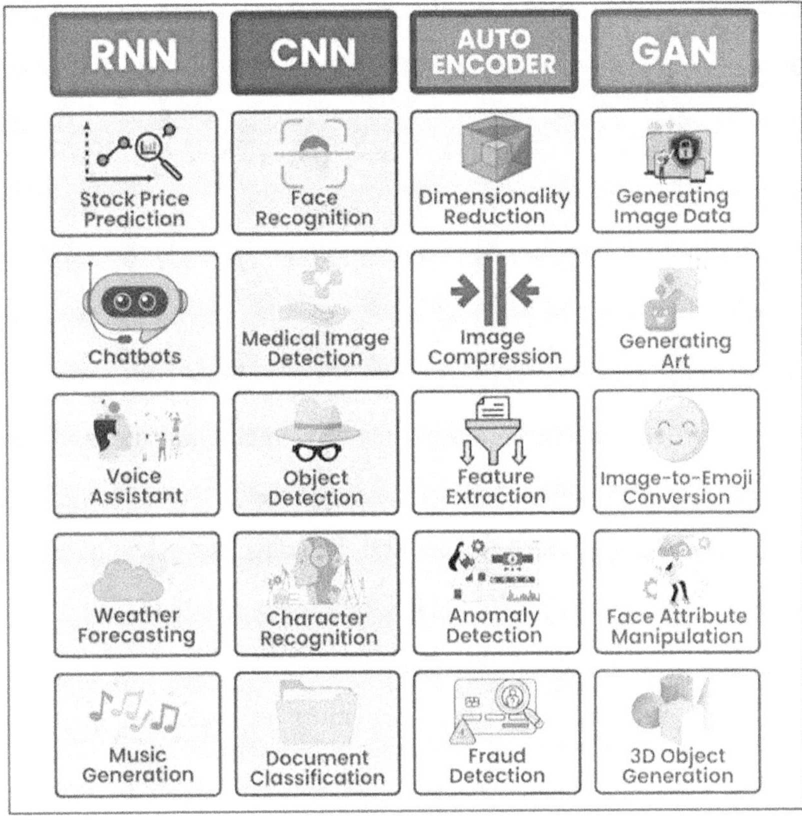



## 6.4 CNNs vs. RNNs

### ❑ CNNs (Convolutional Neural Networks)

*Architecture*: Leverages convolutional layers to capture spatial features from input data.

*Primary Use*: Perfect for tasks like image recognition and object detection.

*Data Input*: Requires fixed-size inputs, ideal for standardized images.

*Memory Handling*: Focuses on spatial data without memory of past inputs.

*Parallelization*: Highly parallelizable, making it efficient for processing.

*Tools:* TensorFlow and PyTorch are widely used for building and training CNNs.

## ❏ RNNs (Recurrent Neural Networks)

*Architecture*: Uses recurrent layers to maintain state, suitable for sequential data.

*Primary Use*: Best for natural language processing, time-series analysis, and other sequential tasks.

*Data Input*: Can handle variable-size inputs and outputs.

*Memory Handling*: Retains memory of previous inputs to process sequences effectively.

*Parallelization*: Less parallelizable due to sequential processing nature.

*Tools*: TensorFlow and PyTorch offer robust support for RNN development and training.

CNNs are optimized for spatial data and excel in visual tasks, while RNNs are designed to manage sequential data, making them essential for language and time-series tasks. The choice between them depends on your project's specific requirements.

| Aspect | CNNs | RNNs |
| --- | --- | --- |
| Architecture | Uses convolutional layers to extract features from data. | Utilizes recurrent layers to process sequential data. |
| Primary Use | Image recognition, computer vision tasks. | Natural language processing, time-series analysis. |
| Data Input | Fixed-size inputs and outputs. | Variable-size inputs and outputs, sequential data handling. |
| Memory Handling | No inherent memory of previous inputs. | Maintains a state (memory) of previous inputs. |
| Parallelization | Highly parallelizable. | Less parallelizable due to sequential processing. |

## 6.5 Deep Learning Optimization

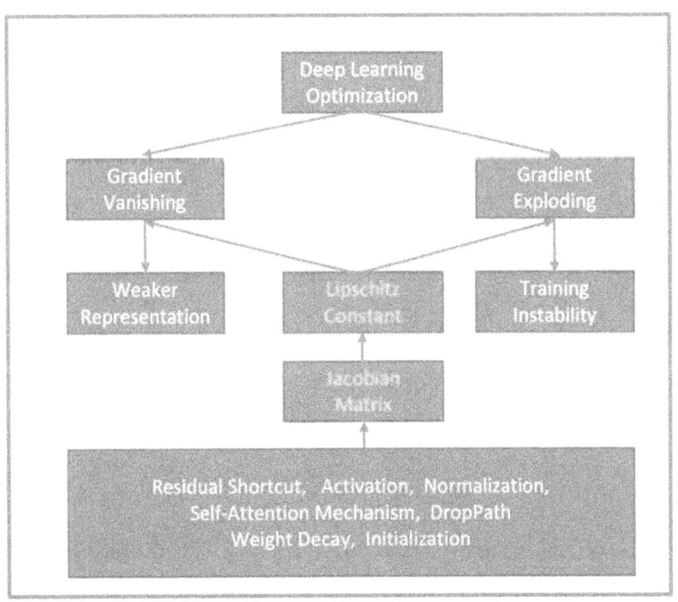

The above figure outlines the key challenges in deep learning optimization and potential solutions.

## Core Problem: Gradient Issues

The central problem highlighted is the instability of gradients during training. This instability manifests in two primary forms:

- ***Gradient Vanishing:*** Gradients become extremely small, hindering the model's ability to learn from past layers. This leads to weaker representations.

- ***Gradient Exploding:*** Gradients become excessively large, causing training instability and divergence.

Both gradient vanishing and exploding negatively impact the Jacobian matrix, which measures the sensitivity of the output to changes in the input. A poorly conditioned Jacobian matrix hampers optimization.

## The Solutions

The bottom of the figure presents techniques designed to address these challenges:

- **Residual Shortcut, Activation, and Normalization:** These methods help stabilize gradients and improve information flow through the network.

- **Self-Attention Mechanism**: This mechanism allows

the model to focus on relevant parts of the input, potentially mitigating gradient issues.

- **DropPath**: A regularization technique that helps prevent overfitting and can indirectly impact gradient stability.

- **Weight Decay, Initialization:** These are standard regularization and initialization methods that contribute to overall training stability.

The figure illustrates the complex interplay between gradient behavior, model performance, and optimization techniques in deep learning. By understanding these challenges and employing appropriate strategies, researchers and practitioners can develop more effective and robust deep-learning models.

## 6.6 AdaGrad in Deep Learning

AdaGrad adjusts the learning rate dynamically for each parameter based on the historical gradient information. This is achieved by maintaining a sum of the squares of the gradients and using this to scale the learning rate.

### Key Formula

The update rule for AdaGrad is:

$$\theta(t+1) = \theta(t) - (\eta / \sqrt{(G(t) + \varepsilon)}) * g(t)$$

Where:

- $\theta(t)$ is the parameter at time step t.

- η is the initial learning rate.

- G(t) is the sum of the squares of the gradients up to time t.

- ε is a small constant to prevent division by zero.

- g(t) is the gradient at time t.

### ○ Advantages

- No manual tuning: Automatically adjusts the learning rate, eliminating the need for manual tuning.

- Faster convergence: Particularly effective in scenarios with sparse data.

- Reliable: More consistent convergence compared to standard SGD.

### ○ Disadvantages

- Decreasing learning rate: The accumulation of squared gradients can cause the learning rate to decrease too much, potentially leading to slow convergence.

### ☐ Use Cases

AdaGrad is well-suited for tasks involving sparse data, such as natural language processing and image recognition, where different features may have varying levels of importance. AdaGrad's adaptive nature makes it a powerful tool in the arsenal of deep learning optimizers.

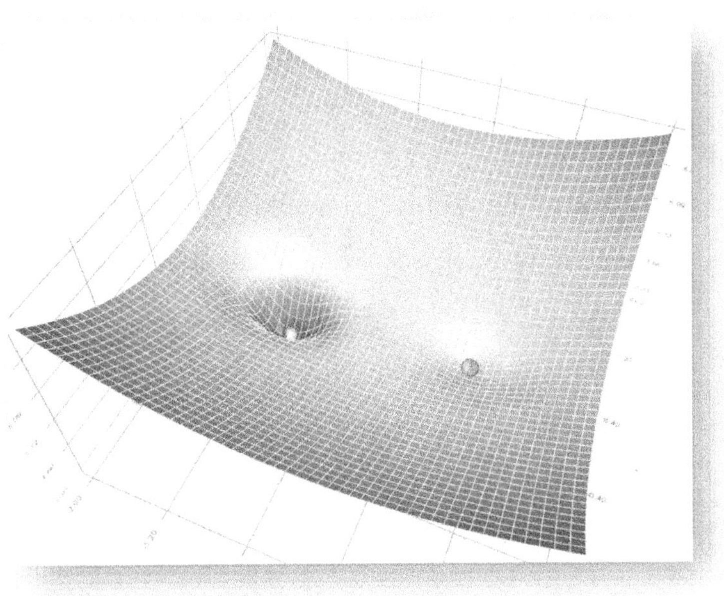

# Chapter 7

# Natural Language Processing (NLP)

(NLP) is a field of artificial intelligence (AI) that focuses on the interaction between computers and human languages. The goal of NLP is to enable machines to understand, interpret, and generate human-like text, and it involves a range of techniques and methods to achieve this. Here's an overview of how NLP works.

❑ Tokenization

- ◉ **Definition:** Tokenization is the process of breaking down a text into smaller units called tokens. Tokens can be words or even characters.

- ◉ **Purpose:** Tokenization provides a structured representation of the input text, making it easier for machines to process and analyze.

❑ Text Cleaning and Preprocessing

- ◉ **Definition:** Text cleaning involves removing irrelevant characters, symbols, and formatting issues from the input text.

- ◉ **Purpose:** Cleaned and preprocessed text ensures that the data is in a standardized form, reducing noise and improving the performance of subsequent NLP tasks.

## Part-of-Speech Tagging

⊙ **Definition:** Part-of-speech tagging involves assigning a grammatical category (such as noun, verb, or adjective) to each word in a sentence.

⊙ **Purpose:** Knowing the parts of speech helps in understanding the syntactic structure of a sentence, which is crucial for many NLP applications.

## Named Entity Recognition (NER)

⊙ **Definition:** NER is the identification and classification of entities (such as names of people, organizations, and locations) within a text.

⊙ **Purpose:** NER helps in extracting and categorizing information from text, which is essential for applications like information retrieval and question answering.

## Syntax and Dependency Parsing

⊙ **Definition:** Syntax parsing involves analyzing the grammatical structure of a sentence and identifying the relationships between words.

⊙ **Purpose:** Syntax parsing helps in understanding the hierarchical structure of sentences, which is useful for various NLP tasks like machine translation and summarization.

## ❑ Word Embeddings

- ◉ **Definition:** Word embeddings are vector representations of words in a continuous vector space.

- ◉ **Purpose:** Word embeddings capture semantic relationships between words. These embeddings are learned from large amounts of text data and are used to represent words in a way that reflects their meaning and context.

## ❑ Machine Learning Models

- ◉ **Definition:** Various machine learning models, such as neural networks, are employed for NLP tasks.

- ◉ **Purpose:** These models are trained on labeled datasets to learn patterns and relationships in language. For example, recurrent neural networks (RNNs) and transformers are commonly used architectures in NLP.

## ❑ Statistical and Probabilistic Models

- ◉ **Definition:** Many NLP tasks involve statistical and probabilistic models, such as Hidden Markov Models (HMMs) or conditional random fields.

⊙ **Purpose:** These models help in making predictions or decisions based on probabilities, often used in tasks like language modeling and speech recognition.

❏ Attention Mechanism

⊙ **Definition:** Attention mechanisms allow models to focus on specific parts of the input sequence when making predictions.

⊙ **Purpose:** Attention mechanisms enhance the ability of models to consider relevant context, which is especially important for tasks involving long sequences of text.

❏ Transfer Learning

⊙ **Definition:** Transfer learning involves pre-training models on large datasets and fine-tuning them for specific tasks.

⊙ **Purpose:** Transfer learning helps leverage knowledge gained from one task or domain to improve performance on another, making it more efficient to train models for specific NLP applications.

❏ Evaluation and Iteration

⊙ **Definition:** NLP models are evaluated using metrics relevant to specific tasks, and the models are iteratively improved based on feedback and performance analysis.

◎ **Purpose:** Continuous evaluation and improvement are essential to refine models and address issues like biases and inaccuracies.

It's important to note that NLP is a dynamic and evolving field, with ongoing research and development aimed at improving the capabilities and addressing challenges such as understanding context, handling ambiguity, and mitigating biases in language models>

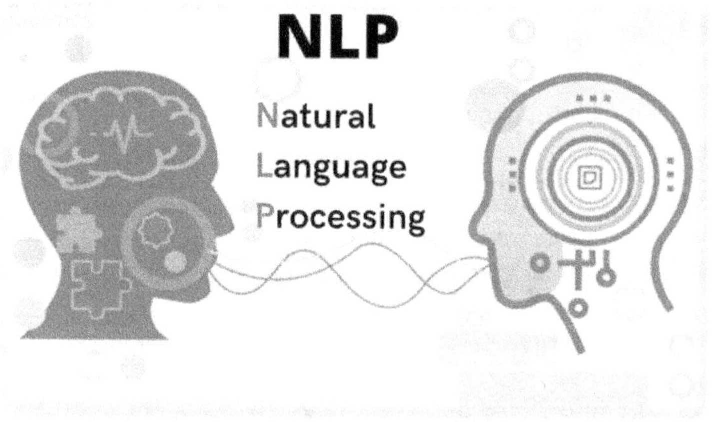


## 7.1  How NLP Works?

NLP systems evaluate vast volumes of unstructured data and extract pertinent information using machine learning methods. The algorithms are taught to identify patterns and draw conclusions from them. This is how it operates:

- The user must input a sentence into the Natural Language Processing (NLP) system.
- The NLP system then breaks down the sentence into smaller parts of words, called tokens, and converts audio to text.
- Then, the machine processes the text data and creates an audio file based on the processed data.
- The machine responds with an audio file based on processed text data.

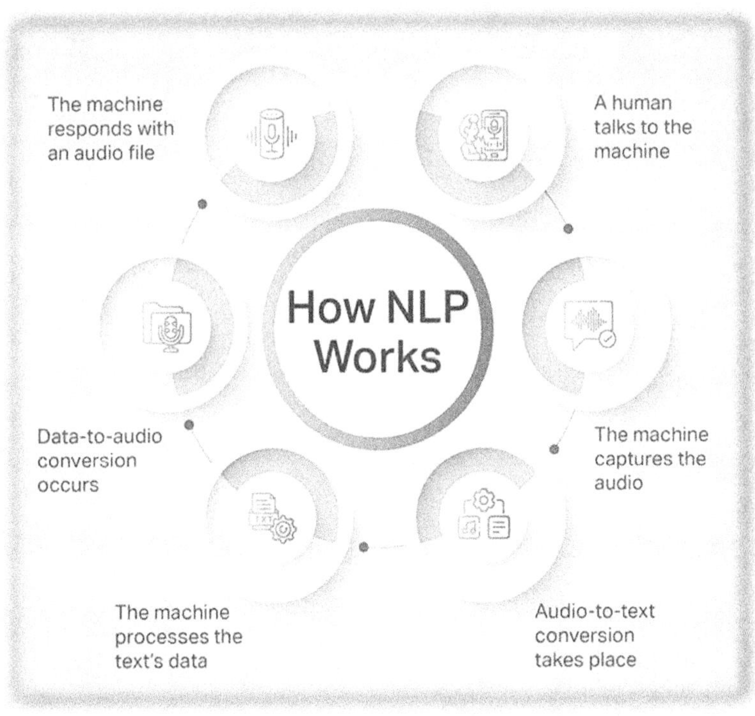

## 7.2  Tasks, Applications, and Future Scope of NLP

❑ Tasks in NLP

#### ◉ Speech Recognition:

This task involves converting spoken language into text. It allows machines to understand and process human speech, enabling applications like voice-activated assistants and transcription services.

#### ◉ Text Classification:

Text classification is the process of categorizing text into predefined categories. It's commonly used for tasks like spam detection, sentiment analysis, and topic categorization.

#### ◉ Language Generation:

Language generation refers to the ability of a model to create coherent and contextually relevant text based on input data. This is essential for applications like automated content creation, chatbots, and text completion.

#### ◉ Language Interaction:

Language interaction encompasses tasks that involve communication between humans and machines using natural language. This includes conversational AI systems like chatbots and virtual assistants that can understand and respond to user inputs.

❑ Applications of NLP

⊙ **Spam Filters:**

NLP is used to sort emails into spam and non-spam categories, helping to keep inboxes free of unwanted messages.

⊙ **Algorithmic Trading:**

NLP can predict stock market trends by analyzing large volumes of text data, such as news articles, social media posts, and financial reports.

⊙ **Question Answering:**

This application involves using NLP to provide accurate answers to questions based on information retrieved from large datasets or the internet.

⊙ **Summarizing Information:**

NLP techniques are employed to condense long documents into shorter summaries, making it easier to digest large amounts of information quickly.

❑ Future Scope of NLP

⊙ **Chatbots:**

The future of NLP includes more advanced chatbots that can assist with inquiries and provide more human-like interactions using natural language processing.

⊙ **Invisible UI:**

NLP will enhance direct communication with machines, allowing users to interact with technology more seamlessly and naturally, without relying on traditional user interfaces.

◉ **Smarter Search:**

Improved search engines that understand and process queries in natural language, providing more accurate and relevant search results.

◉ **Future Enhancements:**

Continued advancements in deep learning and broader language translation have led to more sophisticated and accurate NLP applications that can handle diverse languages and complex tasks.

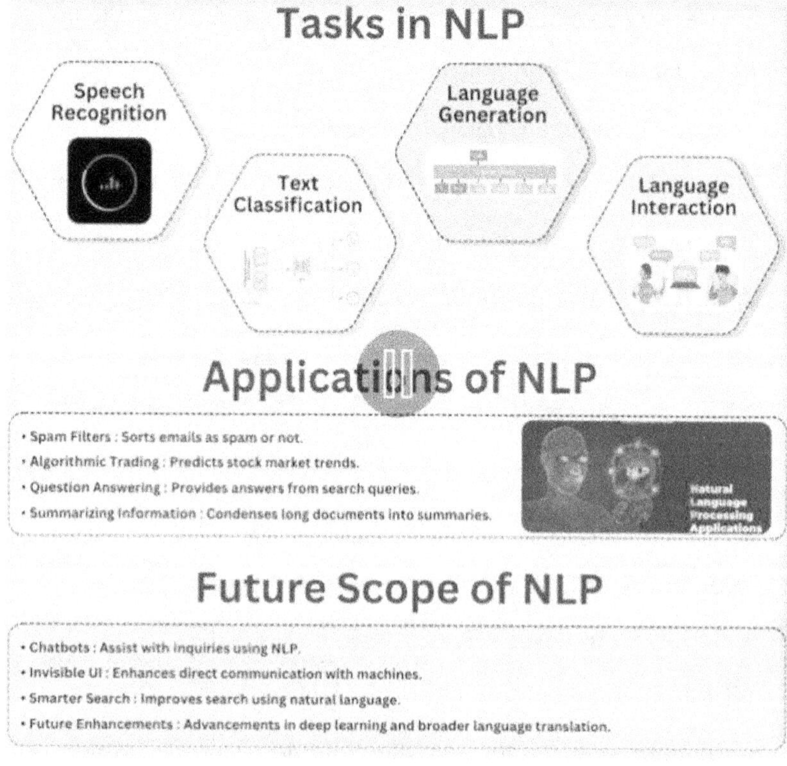

## 7.3 The LLMs Scientist Roadmap

LLMs are AI systems designed to generate human-like text by learning from extensive datasets. They're used for various tasks like translation and conversation. Popular LLMs include GPT (OpenAI), BERT (Google), and Mistral (Mistral AI).

❑ Core Concepts

- Transformer Architecture: Uses attention mechanisms to process text, allowing the model to focus on different parts of the input.

- Tokenization: Breaks text into tokens (words or sub-words) for easier processing.

- Input Representations: Transforms text into vectorized formats to capture meaning and context.

- Attention Mechanisms: Identifies relationships between input tokens to highlight relevant information and manage long-range dependencies.

❑ Transfer Learning and Fine-tuning

- Transfer Learning: Transfers general knowledge from one domain to another, often freezing certain model layers to retain general features.

- Fine-tuning: Adapts the model to specific tasks by adjusting specific layers and re-training parts of the model for targeted training.

❏ Types of LLMs

- Encoder-only models: E.g., BERT, optimized for understanding and processing input data.
- Decoder-only models: E.g., GPT, designed for generating text outputs.
- Encoder-decoder models: E.g., T5, handle tasks involving both input understanding and output generation, useful for translation and summarization.

❏ Preprocessing Techniques

- Text Normalization: Standardizes text by adjusting casing and removing punctuation.
- Stop Words: Removes commonly used words to focus on meaningful content.
- Lemmatization and Stemming: Reduces words to their root form for efficiency.

❏ Applications of LLMs

generative AI solutions like ChatGPT and Google Bard. They enhance search functionalities, customer support, virtual assistants, code development, keyword analysis, and more, driving efficiency and insights across domains.

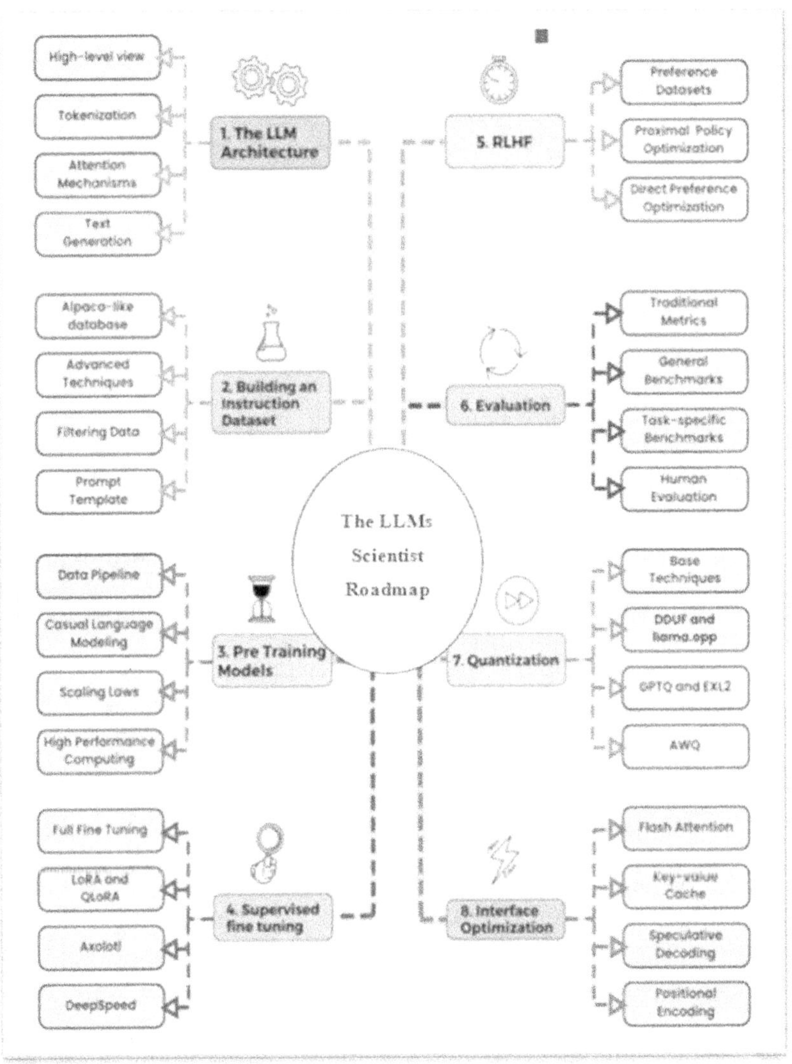


## 7.4  Techniques to Fine-tune LLMs

Here's a breakdown of three techniques: Full Fine-Tuning,
LoRA Fine-Tuning, and RAG (Retrieval-Augmented

Generation):

- ❑ **Complete Fine-Tuning**: This is the traditional method in which all the model's parameters are updated. Although extensive, it may require a lot of resources. Consider it as a complete makeover for your model.

- ❑ **LoRA Fine-Tuning:** LoRA adds a few extra layers and only adjusts them, as opposed to adjusting everything. It can be implemented much more quickly and efficiently. It's like making tactical improvements rather than a complete redesign.

- ❑ **The Recovery-Augmented Generation, or RAG:** This one is a little unique. It blends generation with document retrieval.

To provide more accurate answers to questions, the model retrieves pertinent documents. It works similarly to having a personal research assistant assisting you in the background.

Based on the goal you have in mind, each of these approaches has advantages.

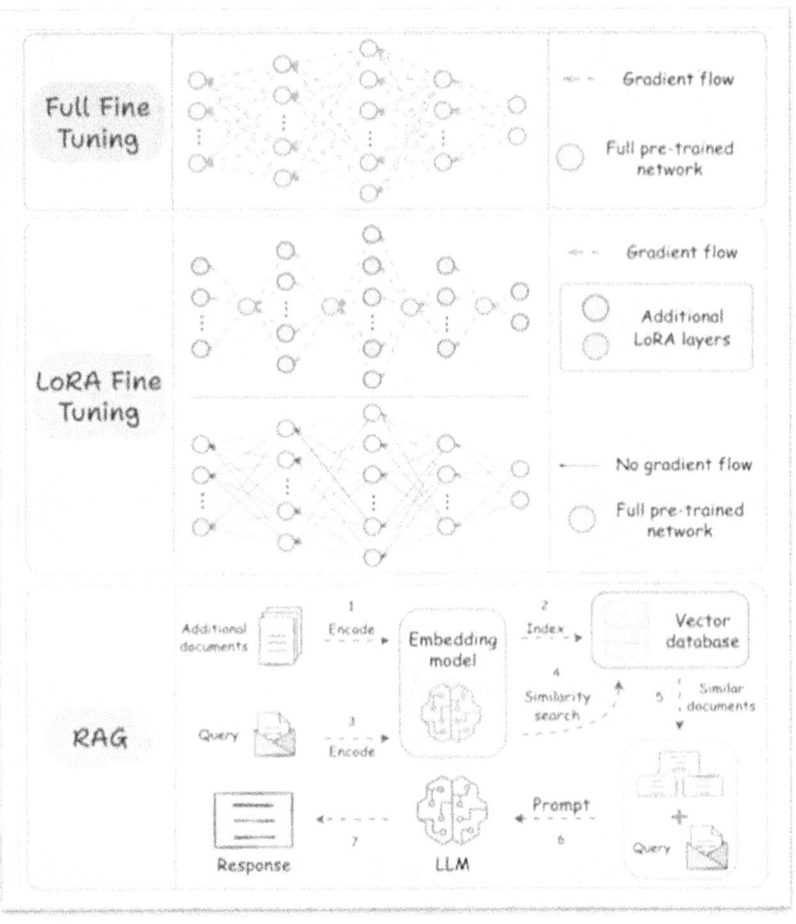


The breakdown for Lora's Fine-tuning is shown in the accompanying figure.

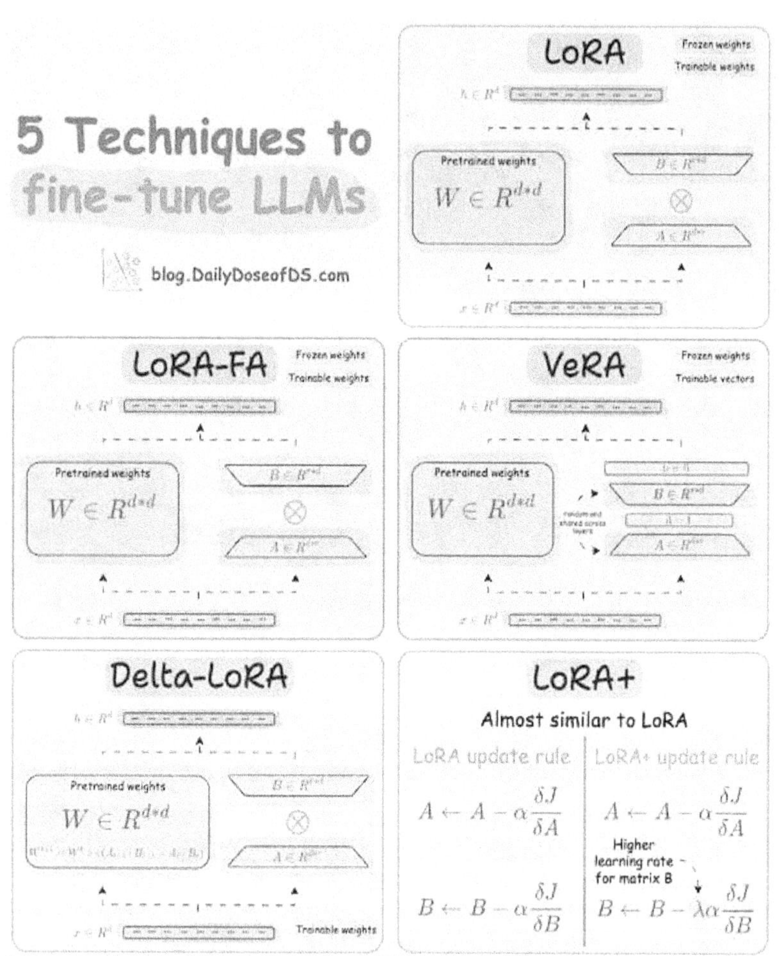


## 7.5  LLMOps vs MLOps

❑ LLMOps (Large Language Roadel Operations)

LLMOps is a specialized subset of MLOps focusing on the operations involved in deploying and maintaining large language models (LLMs) like GPT-4. It addresses the unique challenges posed by the size, complexity, and use cases of LLMs.

## **Key components**

- **Model Scaling:** Managing the resources needed for training and inference of large models.
- **Data Management:** Handling vast amounts of training data and ensuring its quality.
- **Fine-tuning:** Customizing pre-trained models for specific tasks or domains.
- **Deployment:** Efficiently deploying large models to production environments.
- **Monitoring:** Continuously tracking model performance and usage.
- **Ethics and Safety:** Ensuring models are used responsibly and mitigating risks related to bias, misinformation, and other ethical concerns.

## ❑ MLOps (Machine Learning Operations)

MLOps is a set of practices that aims to deploy and maintain machine learning models in production reliably and efficiently. It encompasses the entire lifecycle of machine learning, from data preparation and model training to deployment, monitoring, and governance.

## **Key components**

- **Data Management:** Ensuring data quality, consistency, and availability.
- **Model Training:** Automating and managing the training process.
- **Model Deployment:** Moving models into production environments.
- **Monitoring:** Tracking model performance and detecting issues.
- **Versioning:** Keeping track of data, models, and code versions.
- **Collaboration:** Facilitating teamwork between data scientists, engineers, and stakeholders.

| Feature | LLMOps | MLOps |
| --- | --- | --- |
| Computational resources | Requires more specialized hardware and compute resources | Can be run on a variety of hardware and compute resources |
| Transfer learning | Often uses a foundation model and fine-tunes it with new data | Can be trained from scratch |
| Building LLM chains | Often focuses on building LLM pipelines, rather than building new LLMs | Can focus on either building new models or building pipelines |
| Hyperparameter tuning | Important for reducing the cost and computational power requirements of training | Important for improving accuracy or other metrics |
| Performance metrics | Uses a different set of standard metrics and scoring | Uses well-defined performance metrics, such as accuracy, AUC, F1 score, etc. |
| Prompt engineering | Critical for getting accurate, reliable responses from LLMs | Not as critical, as traditional ML models do not take prompts |

# **Chapter 8**

# Data Visualization

Data visualizations play a crucial role in data analysis because they can effectively condense large datasets into easy-to-understand graphics. There are various types of charts, each with its own advantages and best use cases. One of the most challenging aspects of data analysis is selecting the right chart to represent your data accurately.

When choosing a chart, it's important to first consider what you want the chart to achieve. Common purposes for data visualization include:

- Showing change over time
- Illustrating a part-to-whole relationship
- Depicting flows and processes
- Analyzing data distribution
- Comparing values between groups
- Examining relationships between variables
- Mapping geographical data

Next, think about the type of data you're working with. The choice of the chart will depend on whether your data is categorical, numerical, or a mix of both. Some charts can serve multiple purposes depending on these factors. This book is organized with this method in mind, dedicating each chapter to a different visualization role and covering various chart types suited to common data types and tasks.

## 8.1 How to Choose the Right Graph for Your Project?

The figure below is a decision tree designed to help you select the most appropriate graph for your data visualization needs. It guides you through a series of questions about your data:

❑ Key Questions

- Is your data continuous or categorical? This is the initial split, determining whether your data is numerical (continuous) or represents categories (categorical).

- What is your primary goal? The subsequent questions focus on whether you want to show parts of a whole, trends over time, comparisons, distributions, or relationships between data points.

❑ Graph Types

Based on your answers, the figure suggests suitable graph types:

- ***Categorical data***
  - Parts of a whole: Pie chart
  - Comparisons: Bar chart
  - Distributions: Box and whisker plot, heatmap

- ***Continuous data***
  - Trends over time: Line chart
  - Comparisons: Bar chart, line chart
  - Individual data points: Scatter plot
  - Metric format: Bar chart, box, and whisker plot
  - Relationships: Scatter plot, heatmap
  - Specific format: Spiderweb chart (if applicable)

## ❑ How to Use the Figure?

- Start at the top and answer the questions about your data.
- Follow the branches based on your answers.
- The final node will suggest potential graph types.
- Consider the specific characteristics of your data and visualization goals to make the final choice.

This is a general guide. There might be cases where multiple graph types are suitable, or where a combination of graphs can effectively convey your message.

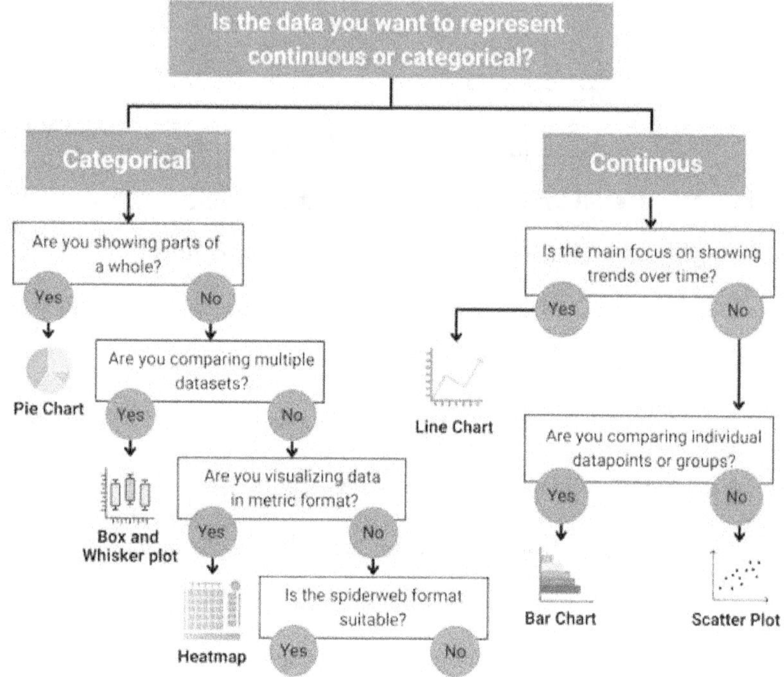


## 8.2  Types of Visualization Graphs

The image below presents a comprehensive overview of various chart types and their applications, The chart is organized into categories based on the type of data and the desired visualization goal.

- *Identify your data type:* Is it categorical (qualitative) or continuous (quantitative)?

- *Determine your visualization goal:* What do you want to show with your data (e.g., trends, comparisons, distributions)?

- *Find the corresponding chart type:* Use the chart to

locate the recommended chart type based on your data and goal.

## ❏ Key Chart Types and Their Uses

- ◉ **Categorical Data:**

  - *Bar Chart:* Compares categories using rectangular bars.

  - *Pie Chart:* Shows proportions of categories as slices of a circle.

  - *Treemap:* Displays hierarchical data using nested rectangles.

  - *Heatmap:* Represents data using color intensity.

  - *Box and Whisker Plot:* Summarizes data distribution and outliers.

- ◉ **Continuous Data:**

  - *Line Chart:* Shows trends over time or across categories.

  - *Scatter Plot:* Plots data points on two axes to identify correlations.

  - *Histogram:* Visualizes data distribution using bins.

  - *Bubble Chart:* Displays three dimensions of data using bubble size.

- *Map:* Represents geographic data.
- *Bullet Chart:* Compares performance against a target.
- *Waterfall Chart:* Visualizes sequential cumulative effect.

## ❏ Additional Considerations

- *Gantt Chart:* Specifically designed for project management, visualizing tasks and timelines.
- *Highlight Table:* Presents tabular data with visual emphasis on specific values.

The best chart type depends on your specific data and the story you want to tell. Experiment with different options to find the most effective visualization.

# Data Scientist Roadmap

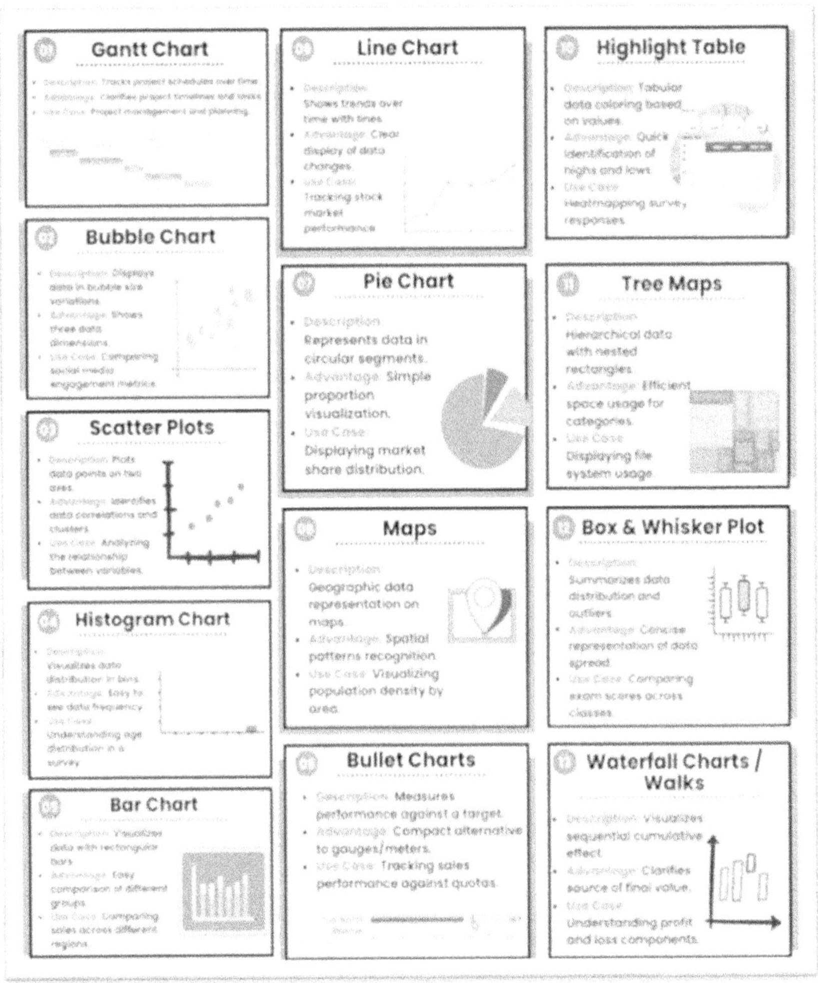

The following picture illustrates some additional chart types that you can depend on when visualizing your data, along with the chart's intended usage and an example of its application:

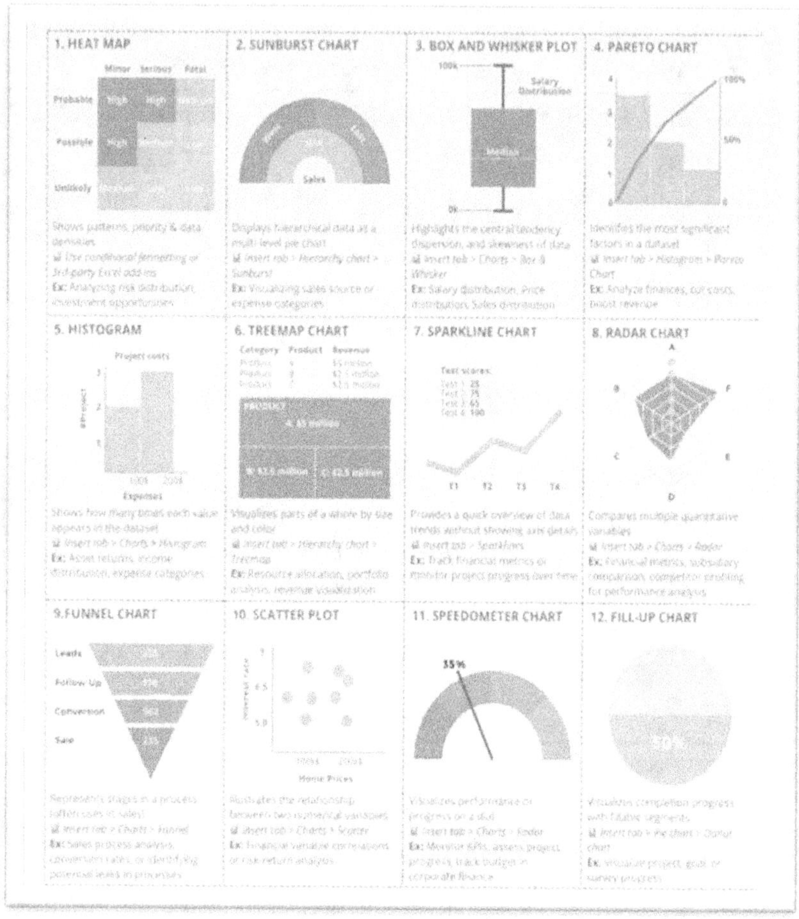

## 8.3  A Guide to Chart Selection

The figure below provides a helpful overview of common chart types and their appropriate use cases.

- ❏ **Chart Selection:** The chart categorizes various chart types based on their suitability for different data scenarios.

❏ ***Data Types:*** The chart differentiates between data that represents quantities (bar charts, line charts) and data that shows proportions or relationships (pie charts, scatter plots).

❏ ***Use Cases:*** For each chart type, the figure provides clear examples of when to use it effectively.

❏ ***Chart Types:***

➢ *Bar Chart:* Best for comparing quantities across categories.

➢ *Line Chart:* Ideal for visualizing trends over time.

➢ *Pie Chart:* Effective for showing proportions and percentages within a whole.

➢ *Scatter Plot:* Useful for identifying relationships and correlations between variables.

➢ *Histogram:* For visualizing the distribution of data.

➢ *Radar Chart:* Suitable for comparing multiple categories across different dimensions.

➢ *Map:* Used to represent geographical data.

➢ *Heatmap:* Effective for visualizing data density and patterns, especially in large datasets.

➢ *Bubble Chart:* For representing three-dimensional data.

➢ *Donut Chart:* Like a pie chart but with a central

hole, often used to emphasize specific parts of a whole.

## ❏ How to Use the Chart?

> ***Identify your data type:*** Determine if your data represents quantities or proportions.

> ***Define your goal:*** Clarify what you want to show with your data (e.g., comparisons, trends, distributions).

> ***Select the appropriate chart:*** Choose the chart type that best aligns with your data and goal based on the provided guidelines.

By following these steps, you can effectively select the right chart to communicate your data clearly and effectively.

| Chart | Types of Chart | When to use it | Example of Use Cases |
|---|---|---|---|
| | Bar Chart | Compare quantities across Categories | Compare sales of different products. |
| | Line Chart | Show Trends over time | Display the growth of website traffic over a year. |
| | Pie Chart | Highlight proportions and percentages | Illustrate the breakdown of expenses in a budget. |
| | Scatter Plot | Represent relationships between variables | Identify correlations between marketing spend and ROI. |
| | Histogram | Visualize the distribution of data | Show the age distribution of survey respondents. |
| | Radar Chart | Compare multiple categories across dimensions | Evaluate the performance of a product in various areas. |
| | Map | Visualize geospatial data | Display regional sales performance on a map. |
| | Heatmap | Visualize data density and patterns especially in large data set | Identifying hotspots of customer activity in a shopping mall. |
| | Bubble Chart | Represent three-dimensional data | Compare revenue, cost, and profit in three dimensions. |
| | Donut Chart | Emphasize specific parts within a whole | Show the distribution of marketing expenditures. |

## 8.4  Most Important Plots in Data Science

There are compilations of key plots commonly used in data science. These plots are essential tools for exploratory data analysis, model evaluation, and feature engineering.

The Plot Categories depend on their Purposes:

❑ Model Evaluation

- ◉ *ROC Curve:* Visualizes the performance of a classification model by plotting the true positive rate against the false positive rate.

- ◉ *KS Plot:* Compares the cumulative distribution functions of two groups (e.g., target classes) to assess model performance.

- ◉ *SHAP Plot:* Explains the impact of features on model predictions.

- ◉ *Precision-Recall Plot:* Evaluates the trade-off between precision and recall in classification models.

❑ Data Exploration and Visualization

- ◉ *QQ Plot (Quantile-Quantile Plot):* Compares the distribution of a dataset to a theoretical distribution (often normal).

- ◉ *Elbow Curve:* Helps determine the optimal number of clusters in clustering algorithms.

- ◉ *Silhouette Curve:* Evaluates the quality of clustering results by measuring how similar a data point is to its own cluster compared to other clusters.

- *Partial Dependency Plot:* Shows the marginal effect of a feature on the predicted outcome.

❏ Model Understanding and Improvement

- *Cumulative Explained Variance Plot:* Visualizes the amount of variance explained by each principal component in PCA.
- *Gini Impurity vs. Entropy:* Compares two impurity measures used in decision trees.
- *Bias-Variance Tradeoff:* Illustrates the relationship between model complexity, bias, and variance.

By understanding these plots and their applications, data scientists can effectively explore data, build robust models, and interpret results.

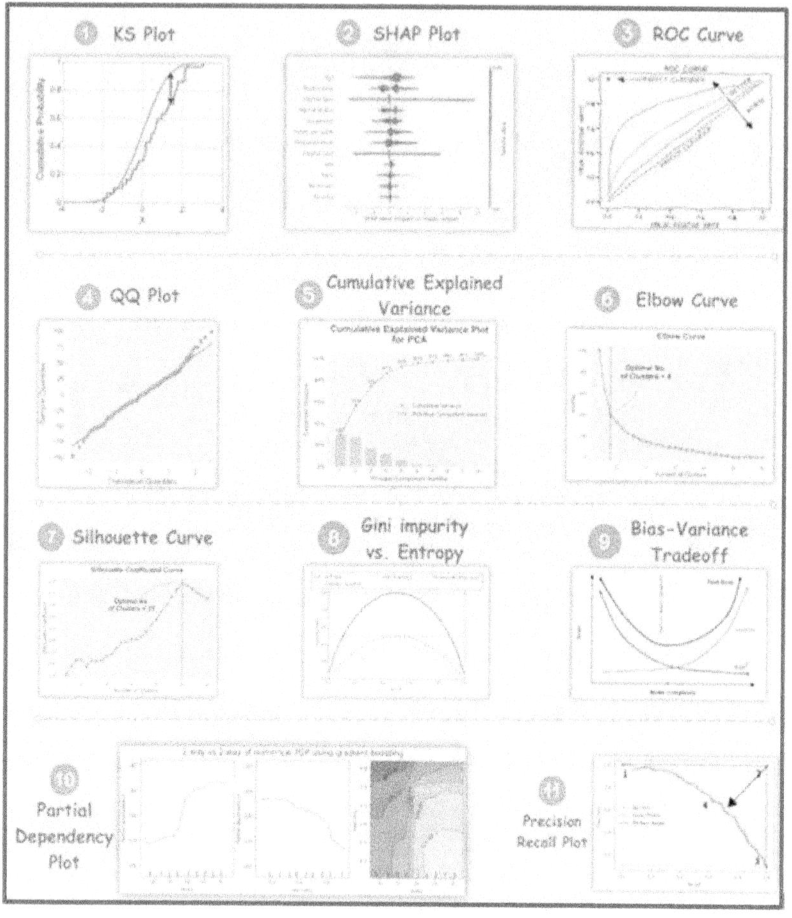

## 8.5  Visualization based on Objective

The Figure below contains a categorizing of different chart types based on their purpose.

It groups charts into categories:

- ✓ Raw Number: For displaying single values or comparisons.

# Data Scientist Roadmap

✓ **Part-to-Whole**: For visualizing proportions within a whole.

✓ **Relationship**: For showing connections between variables.

✓ **Change over Time**: For tracking data over time.

✓ **Distribution**: For understanding data spread.

✓ **Geospatial**: For mapping data on geographic locations.

Each category includes specific chart types with brief descriptions.

# Chapter 9

# Deployment

## 9.1 Microsoft Azure

*Microsoft-developed computing platform. Through its worldwide infrastructure, it provides administration, access, and creation of applications and services to people, businesses, and governments. Moreover, it offers several functions, such as platform as a service (PaaS), infrastructure as a service (IaaS), and software as a service (SaaS). A wide range of programming languages, tools, and frameworks are supported by Microsoft Azure, along with third-party and Microsoft-specific apps and services.*

| | |
|---|---|
| **Developer (s)** | Microsoft |
| **Initial release** | October 27, 2008; 15 years ago, |
| **Operating system** | Linux, Microsoft Windows, macOS, iOS, Android |

| Type | Web service, cloud computing |
| --- | --- |
| **License** | Proprietary for platform, MIT License for client SDKs |
| **Website** | azure.microsoft.com |

It allows developers to build sites using ASP.NET, PHP, Node.js, Java, or Python, which can be deployed using FTP, Git, Mercurial, Team Foundation Server, or uploaded through the user portal. This feature was announced in preview form in June 2012 at the Meet Microsoft Azure event.[12] Customers can create websites in PHP, ASP.NET,

Microsoft Azure provides two deployment strategies for cloud resources: the Azure Resource Manager and the "classic" model. Previously, every resource, such as a virtual machine or SQL database, needed to be managed independently. However, Azure launched the Azure Resource Manager in 2014, enabling customers to organize related services into groups. Resources that

## 9.2  Heroku

# HEROKU

*Heroku is a cloud platform as a service (PaaS) supporting several programming languages. As one of the first cloud platforms, Heroku has been in development since June 2007, when it supported only the Ruby programming language, but now also supports Java, Node.js, Scala, Clojure, Python, PHP, and Go. For this reason, Heroku is said to be a polyglot platform as it has features for a developer to build, run and scale applications in a similar manner across most of these languages. Heroku was acquired by Salesforce in 2010 for $212 million.*

| | |
|---|---|
| **Company Type** | Subsidiary |
| **Industry** | Cloud platform as a service |
| **Founded** | 2007; 17 years ago, |
| **Founder** | James Lindenbaum, Adam Wiggins, Orion Henry |
| **Headquarters** | San Francisco, California |
| **Key people** | Bob Wise (CEO), Gail Frederick (CTO) |
| **Products** | Heroku Platform, Heroku Postgres, Heroku Redis, Heroku Enterprise, Heroku Teams, Heroku Connect, Heroku Elements, Heroku Review Apps |
| **Parent** | Salesforce.com |
| **Website** | heroku.com |

The Heroku network runs the customer's apps in virtual containers which execute on a reliable runtime environment. Heroku calls these containers "Dynos". These Dynos can run code written in Node, Ruby, PHP, Go, Scala, Python, Java, or Clojure. Heroku also provides custom build packs with which the developer can deploy apps in any other language. Heroku lets the developer scale the app instantly just by either increasing the number of dynos or by changing the type of

## 9.3  Google Cloud Platform

Google Cloud Platform (GCP) is a suite of cloud computing services offered by Google that provides a series of modular cloud services including computing, data storage, data analytics, and machine learning, alongside a set of management tools. It runs on the same infrastructure that Google uses internally for its end-user products, such as Google Search, Gmail, and Google Docs, according to Verma et al. Registration requires a credit card or bank

| Owner | **Google** |
|---|---|
| Industry | Web service, cloud computing |
| Revenue | US$33.1 billion (2023) |

| | |
|---|---|
| Operating income | US$1.72 billion (2023) |
| URL | cloud.google.com |
| Launched | April 7, 2008; 16 years ago, |
| Status | Active |
| Written in | <ul><li>Java</li><li>C++</li><li>Python</li><li>Go</li><li>Ruby</li></ul> |

Google Cloud Platform provides infrastructure as a service, platform as a service, and serverless computing environments.

Google Cloud Platform is a part of Google Cloud, which includes the Google Cloud Platform public cloud infrastructure, as well as Google Workspace (G Suite), enterprise versions of Android and ChromeOS, and application programming interfaces (APIs) for machine learning and enterprise mapping services.

Google lists over 100 products under the Google Cloud brand such as **computing, Storage and databases, Networking, Big data, Cloud AI, Management tools, Internet of Things (IoT), API platforms.**

## 9.4  Flask

*Flask is a micro web framework written in Python. It is classified as a microframework because it does not require tools or libraries. It has no database abstraction layer, form validation, or any other components where pre-existing third-party libraries provide common functions. However, Flask supports extensions that can add application features as if they were implemented in Flask itself. Extensions exist*

| | |
|---|---|
| **Developer(s)** | Armin Ronacher |
| **Initial release** | April 1, 2010; 14 years ago, |
| **Stable release** | 7 April 2024; 4 months ago, |
| **Repository** | github.com/pallets/flask |
| **Written in** | Python |
| **Type** | Web framework |
| **License** | BSD 3-clause license |
| **Website** | palletsprojects.com/p/flask/ |

- Development server and debugger
- Integrated support for unit testing
- RESTful request dispatching
- Uses Jinja templating
- Support for secure cookies (client-side sessions)
- 100% WSGI 1.0 compliant
- Unicode-based
- Complete documentation
- Google App Engine compatibility
- Extensions available to extend functionality

## 9.5 Django

# django

sometimes stylized as django is a free and open-source, Python-based web framework that runs on a web server. It follows the model–template–views (MTV) architectural pattern. It is maintained by the Django Software Foundation (DSF), an independent organization established in the US as a 501(c)(3) non-profit.

| | |
|---|---|
| **Original author(s)** | Adrian Holovaty, Simon Willison |
| **Developer(s)** | Django Software Foundation |
| **Initial release** | 21 July 2005; 19 years ago, |

| | |
|---|---|
| **Stable release** | 9 July 2024; 33 days ago, |
| **Repository** | github.com/Django/Django |
| **Written in** | Python |
| **Size** | 8.9 MB |
| **Type** | Web framework |
| **License** | 3-clause BSD |
| **Website** | www.djangoproject.com |

Django's primary goal is to ease the creation of complex, database-driven websites. The framework emphasizes reusability and "pluggability" of components, less code, low coupling, rapid development, and the principle of don't repeat yourself. Python is used throughout, even for settings, files, and data models. Django also provides an optional administrative create, read, update, and delete interface that is generated dynamically through introspection and configured via admin models.

## 9.6 Examples of the Data Science Projects

| # | Project Name | # | Project Name |
| --- | --- | --- | --- |
| 1 | Housing Price Predictor | 51 | Complaint Analyzer |
| 2 | Customer Segmentation | 52 | Hospital Readmission Predictor |
| 3 | Fraud Detection | 53 | Equipment Fault Detector |
| 4 | Movie Recommender | 54 | News Feed Recommender |
| 5 | Stock Price Predictor | 55 | Outbreak Predictor |
| 6 | Churn Predictor | 56 | Network Analyzer |
| 7 | Sentiment Analysis | 57 | Hotel Booking Predictor |
| 8 | Image Classifier | 58 | Activity Recognizer |
| 9 | Credit Risk Analysis | 59 | Ticket Classifier |
| 10 | Email Spam Detector | 60 | Crop Yield Predictor |
| 11 | Disease Diagnosis | 61 | Mask Detector |
| 12 | E-commerce Recommender | 62 | Reputation Analyzer |
| 13 | Text Summarizer | 63 | Social Media Event Detector |
| 14 | Weather Forecaster | 64 | Image Describer |
| 15 | Visitor Predictor | 65 | User Engagement Predictor |
| 16 | Flight Delay Predictor | 66 | Event Recommender |

| # | Project Name | # | Project Name |
| --- | --- | --- | --- |
| 17 | Handwritten Digit Recognizer | 67 | Defect Detector |
| 18 | Lifetime Value Predictor | 68 | Purchase Behavior Analyzer |
| 19 | Loan Default Predictor | 69 | Store Sales Predictor |
| 20 | Autonomous Navigation | 70 | Conservation Monitor |
| 21 | Employee Attrition Predictor | 71 | Air Quality Predictor |
| 22 | Traffic Flow Predictor | 72 | Response Time Predictor |
| 23 | Music Genre Classifier | 73 | Market Trend Analyzer |
| 24 | Object Detector | 74 | Document Classifier |
| 25 | Fashion Recognizer | 75 | Dropout Predictor |
| 26 | Employee Performance Predictor | 76 | Fake Account Detector |
| 27 | Food Recognizer | 77 | Personality Predictor |
| 28 | Solar Power Predictor | 78 | Product Demand Predictor |
| 29 | Product Review Analyzer | 79 | Image Segmented |
| 30 | Traffic Anomaly | 80 | Topic Modeler |

| # | Project Name | # | Project Name |
|---|---|---|---|
|  | Detector |  |  |
| 31 | Shelf Space Optimizer | 81 | Movie Genre Classifier |
| 32 | Service Time Predictor | 82 | Speech Emotion Recognizer |
| 33 | Credit Card Fraud Predictor | 83 | E-commerce Sales Forecaster |
| 34 | Ticket Sales Predictor | 84 | Intrusion Detector |
| 35 | Text-to-Speech Converter | 85 | Restaurant Recommender |
| 36 | Demographic Segmentation | 86 | Movie Sentiment Analyzer |
| 37 | Price Optimizer | 87 | Emotion Detector |
| 38 | Inventory Demand Predictor | 88 | Stock News Media Analyzer |
| 39 | Congestion Predictor | 89 | Logistics Identifier |
| 40 | Turnover Predictor | 90 | Sales Price Predictor |
| 41 | Disease Spread Predictor | 91 | Salary Predictor |
| 42 | Speech-to-Text Converter | 92 | Customer Satisfaction Analyzer |
| 43 | Road Condition Monitor | 93 | Video Classifier |

| # | Project Name | # | Project Name |
|---|---|---|---|
| 44 | Taxi Demand Predictor | 94 | Student Performance Predictor |
| 45 | Passenger Demand Forecaster | 95 | Face Recognizer |
| 46 | Playlist Generator | 96 | Energy Predictor |
| 47 | Burnout Predictor | 97 | Fake News Classifier |
| 48 | Poaching Detector | 98 | Traffic Sign Recognizer |
| 49 | Energy Consumption Predictor | 99 | Playlist generator |
| 50 | Threat Detector | 100 | Cyberbullying Detector |

## 9.7   Recommendations for Data Scientists

- **Programming Languages:** Start with the basics—Python, R, and SQL. These are the backbone of data science, enabling data manipulation, analysis, and querying.

- **Mathematics & Statistics:** Strengthen your foundation with Linear Algebra, Probability & Statistics, and Calculus—critical for understanding data patterns and building models.

- Data Handling: Learn the art of data collection, cleaning, wrangling, and transformation to prepare raw data for analysis.

● ***Exploratory Data Analysis (EDA):*** Master descriptive statistics, data profiling, correlation analysis, and outlier detection to uncover hidden insights.

● ***Data Visualization:*** Visualize data effectively with tools like Matplotlib, Seaborn, Tableau, and Power BI to communicate findings.

● ***Machine Learning Basics:*** Delve into supervised and unsupervised learning, including regression, classification, clustering, and model evaluation.

● ***Advanced Analytics:*** Enhance your analytical skills with predictive modeling, time series analysis, text analytics, and sentiment analysis.

● ***Data Engineering:*** Get hands-on with ETL processes, data warehousing, and big data tools like Hadoop and Spark to manage large datasets.

● ***Databases & SQL:*** Build expertise in relational databases, advanced SQL queries, and database management.

● ***Big Data Technologies:*** Explore big data technologies like Hadoop, Spark, and Hive to process and analyze massive datasets.

● ***Business Intelligence:*** Leverage dashboards, KPI

tracking, business reporting, and data-driven decision-making for strategic insights.

- *Cloud Platforms:* Learn cloud computing with AWS, Azure, and Google Cloud to manage and deploy data science projects at scale.

- *Experiment Tracking:* Track your experiments with MLflow and Weights & Biases to ensure reproducibility and efficient model management.

- *Version Control Systems:* Use Git and platforms like GitHub/GitLab to manage code, collaborate, and track project changes.

- *Data Ethics:* Understand the importance of bias, fairness, data privacy, and transparency in data science.

- *Communication & Storytelling:* Master data narratives, visualization, presentation skills, and stakeholder communication to tell compelling data stories.

# ABOUT THE AUTHOR

Mohammed M. Ahmed is a Ph.D. candidate in business analytics at Bahrain University. He holds a B.Sc. in mathematics from the University of Bahrain and an M.Sc. in human resources management (HRM) from Applied Science University (AUS) in Bahrain. His research interests include machine learning, MATH, and Human resources. He is currently working as the head of the human resources planning department.

https://orcid.org/0009-0009-0658-6958

phdmohammed114@gmail.com